The Communication Manifesto

T0048672

The Manifesto Series

David Buckingham, *The Media Education Manifesto*
Silvio Waisbord, *The Communication Manifesto*

Silvio Waisbord

The Communication Manifesto

polity

The right of Silvio Waisbord to be identified as Author of this Work has been asserted in accordance with the UK Copyright, Designs and Patents Act 1988.

First published in 2020 by Polity Press

Polity Press
65 Bridge Street
Cambridge CB2 1UR, UK

Polity Press
101 Station Landing
Suite 300
Medford, MA 02155, USA

ISBN-13: 978-1-5095-3219-3
ISBN-13: 978-1-5095-3220-9 (pb)

A catalogue record for this book is available from the British Library.

Library of Congress Cataloging-in-Publication Data
Names: Waisbord, Silvio R. (Silvio Ricardo), 1961- author.
Title: The communication manifesto / Silvio Waisbord.
Description: Cambridge, UK ; Medford, MA : Polity Press, [2019] | Series: Manifesto series | Includes bibliographical references. |
Identifiers: LCCN 2019011786 (print) | LCCN 2019017099 (ebook) | ISBN 9781509532223 (Epub) | ISBN 9781509532193 (hardback) | ISBN 9781509532209 (pbk.)
Subjects: LCSH: Communication--Philosophy.
Classification: LCC P90 (ebook) | LCC P90 .W2185 2019 (print) | DDC 302.23--dc23
LC record available at https://lccn.loc.gov/2019011786

Typeset in 11 on 15 Sabon by
Servis Filmsetting Ltd, Stockport, Cheshire
Printed and bound in the UK by CPI Group (UK) Ltd, Croydon

For further information on Polity, visit our website: politybooks.com

Contents

Acknowledgments

I am grateful to Mary Savigar for the invitation to contribute to Polity's series on manifestos in communication and media studies. Her invitation came as I was completing my book on the state of communication studies, also with Polity. The offer was appealing yet daunting. It was an opportunity to develop ideas I had been thinking through for a while, even if the suggested title, *The Communication Manifesto*, with echoes of Marx and Engels' masterpiece of the manifesto genre, was intimidating. Also, writing a manifesto, as "poeticized action" in Tristan Tzara's (1981) definition, was not in my wheelhouse. Prescriptive, action-oriented, rousing briefs were not the preferred style of my written scholarship. I have been more inclined to dissect media and communication questions and parse academic arguments than to urge colleagues

Acknowledgments

to take political action. Eventually, I enthusiastically accepted Mary's offer after concluding that the manifesto genre is suitable to make an argument for why communication studies needs to step up interventions with non-academic publics.

I have been intrigued about the role of intellectuals in public life since reading Karl Mannheim's *Ideology and Utopia* for a sociological theory course in college in 1979, during the last military dictatorship in Argentina. Reading Mannheim's argument in favor of public intellectualism while I was living under authoritarianism was a jarring and critical moment (perhaps not exactly the intention of the faculty, who had been appointed by the regime). The dictatorship persecuted, tortured, and disappeared intellectuals, scholars, and scientists who were engaged in dissident politics and had worked with political parties, unions, alternative media, guerrilla movements, low-income communities, and social movements. In my mind, Mannheim's argument endorsed the idea, well established in Latin American intellectual history, that scholars should be actively involved in public affairs beyond the classroom. Knowledge is socially and politically grounded, he argued. My academic surroundings proved his point, even amid military repression of critical thinking. Politics infused virtually everything – curricula, classroom discussions, faculty appointments – before, during, and after the dictatorship. Once the pro-democracy movement gained ascendancy, students' activism ran high in the streets and university politics. In this context, it was natural to wonder about one's position in public life, even as a budding scholar.

I continued to ponder these issues after I moved to the United States in the late 1980s and throughout my academic career. These matters became more concrete after I left academia to work on communication research and practice in international development. I regularly collaborated with government agencies, civic society organizations, scientists and technical experts, and activists' groups. Although this book is not a memoir, it gave me the opportunity to take stock of my thoughts and experiences.

The focus of the book is on public scholarship in communication studies: interventions by communication scholars in the public sphere beyond academic campuses. If manifestos are part sermon, part technical guide, as Terry Eagleton (2017) wonderfully put it, this manifesto hopes to be the latter more than the former. As a reader, I never found the high-minded tone of manifestos engaging, although some examples, notably Thomas Paine's

Acknowledgments

Common Sense as well as the pamphlets by early twentieth-century artistic vanguards, were hugely formative readings. Like any manifesto, this book makes a normative argument and offers recommendations with the hope to influence conversations and actions.

I benefited from "conversations with a purpose" (Burgess, 1988) with friends and colleagues, many of whom represent the kind of public scholarship that communication studies embraces and should fully support. Special thanks to Amit Schejter, Andrea Palopoli, Bob McChesney, Carmen Gonzalez, Carolyn Bryerly, Carrie Rentschler, Cherian George, Chris Anderson, Claudia Lagos, Dafna Lemish, Eduardo Villanueva, George Villanueva, Holley Wilkin, Iccha Basnyat, Jacqueline Vickery, Jair Vega, Karla Palma, Kate Wright, Larry Gross, Lisa Henderson, Lynn Schofield Clark, Maria Soledad Segura, Martha Fuentes, Michael Delli Carpini, Pablo Boczkowski, Pat Aufderheide, Paula Gardner, Peter Lemish, Phil Napoli, Ralina Joseph, Rasmus Nielsen, Sandra Osses, Sarah Stonbely, Seth Noar, Sonia Livingstone, Stephen Ostertag, Stine Eckert, Talia Stroud, and Vikki Katz. Our conversations helped me to a better understanding of opportunities and challenges for public scholarship, as well as the ways communication studies contributes to

Acknowledgments

a better informed and more egalitarian and tolerant world.

Thanks to Sarah Dicioccio for her excellent assistance with various aspects of this book. I am grateful to Ellen MacDonald-Kramer, Justin Dyer, and everyone else at Polity for their support throughout the process. Two reviewers offered thoughtful feedback.

Introduction

Calls for public scholarship have been frequent in the social sciences and the humanities in recent years. Influential voices across the disciplines have urged colleagues to utilize their expertise for the betterment of society and warned about the problems of producing knowledge exclusively for fellow academics (Burawoy, 2005; Calhoun, 2004; Oakes, 2018). Communication scholars, too, have made similar appeals to contribute to society, social justice, and communication professions (Dempsey et al., 2011; Rosen, 1995). These appeals reflect two issues. One is the recognition that not enough is done to make academic knowledge socially significant and impactful: to help societies understand and address a host of problems by tapping into accumulated knowledge (Bastow, Dunleavy & Tinkler, 2014; Hanemaayer & Schneider, 2015). The other issue is growing concerns about the (ir)relevance of academic disciplines and knowledge (Flinders, 2013; Hoffman, 2016; Peters, Pierre & Stoker, 2014) in society at large. If scholars do not take the question of social relevance seriously, academic scholarship runs the risk of remaining important for scholars, but unrecognized or, worse, dismissed by society.

Calls for public scholarship have sparked much conversation and soul-searching, as reflected in the themes of scores of panels and publications. It seems that virtually everyone believes public scholarship matters. It is hard to imagine anyone would say otherwise. I haven't heard anyone proudly affirming in a big public forum: "Stick to conventional scholarship and forget society or contributing to the social good." There are no two neatly defined, warring camps about public scholarship: those in favor and their opponents entangled in a battle over the soul and the purpose of academe (see Mulholland, 2015). Public scholarship is generally praised without much vocal opposition. It is unclear, however, whether rousing calls for action have resulted in large-scale, concrete, and sustainable actions that have turned public scholarship into a central aspect of academia. The irony should not be overlooked: without effective action, calls for public scholarship may generate additional scholarship, in the form of publications, courses, and symposia, but the actual impact on society may be negligible.

In this book, I make a call for public scholarship in communication studies with the hope of contributing ideas to conversations and actions. Academics should contribute to society in more ways than by producing knowledge and exchanging ideas with students and fellow scholars. *Contra* conservative thinkers, who have generally bemoaned the public role of intellectuals, I believe communication scholars make important, unique contributions to public life. By bringing a wide range of expertise and skills, they collaborate with actors and communities in efforts to improve public life and make societies more tolerant, informed, empathetic, egalitarian. Their actions reflect a concern with addressing real-world problems rather than only dealing with typical scholarly questions about theories, methodologies, arguments, and so on. They represent a gradual shift in the gravitational center of scholarship to highlight what Rasmus Nielsen (2018, p. 147) calls "context-driven, problem-focused, and interdisciplinary forms of knowledge production." So what is needed is to link knowledge production with practice by understanding the causes of communication and social problems in specific

3

settings, identifying possible solutions, producing evidence-based analysis and recommendations, and supporting collective competencies and actions.

The vision of public scholarship presented here differs from conventional notions that believe interventions beyond academia are limited to the models of the public intellectual and the scholar-activist. These models, I argue, are two possibilities among a range of possible performative and normative positions scholars take. The model of the public intellectual is linked to the view that scholars are members of the "republic/men of letters" who impart wisdom and guidance to elites and the masses – those who, in the words of Mannheim (1936, pp. 142–143), "provide an interpretation of the world ... in what otherwise would be a pitch-black night." Even if some scholars fit this model, as they make forays into the news media, public scholarship is not synonymous with "public intellectualism." The latter has analytical and normative problems for comprehending the multiple connections between communication studies, public life, and social justice. The model of the scholar-activist is also only one option for public scholarship. Just as there is no single model of scholarship in communication studies, public scholarship also takes different shapes: community-embedded scholars, armchair activists, expert contributors, part-time advocates, long-distance sympathizers, prominent talking heads, pugnacious militants, experienced practitioners, committed scientists. Hopefully, this book will contribute to reshaping the way we view public scholarship.

I believe a communication approach sensitive to the plurality of spaces, publics, and positions linking academia and society is necessary to broaden understandings of public scholarship. We should not espouse a media-centric understanding of public scholarship. The critique of media-centric analysis reminds us that communication continues to take place in everyday spaces where social and political life and scholarship happen. In media-obsessed, celebrity-struck societies, oftentimes scholars are also similarly in awe of intellectual marquee names with a regular media presence. We should not equate public scholarship with media appearances. Nor should we think that it only takes place in the public spaces of street activism: rallies, marches, teach-ins, and barricades. We need to acknowledge that it happens in a range of arenas: schools, community centers, government offices, civic organizations, radio stations, zines, newsrooms, and workplaces.

I also hope the book informs debates about public scholarship in communication studies and developing concrete actions in support of public scholars. I feel that debates often take place among scholars who already believe public scholarship matters: communities of knowledge defined by long-standing collaborations with governments and civic organizations, activist stands, and/or particular ideological and theoretical convictions. As important as they are, we need to reach a wider public within and outside communication studies. We need to raise awareness, spark discussion, and promote changes among the unaware, the uninitiated, the misinformed, and the skeptics. Otherwise, public scholarship may remain a thematic priority among only a slice of communication scholars. Many colleagues (especially junior scholars), with spirited conviction and supported by fellow travelers, realize that public scholarship is widely praised but not solidly supported by all universities. They quickly find out that it presents many challenges. Building relations with non-academic actors, going through many bureaucratic hoops to get approval by universities and partners, and juggling multiple demands are time-consuming activities. Moving to action is not so simple, given the tensions between high-minded praise for public scholarship and the customary pressures of scholarship, in-group support, and lack of attention (or, worse, punishment) from university administrations and colleagues.

Finally, I intend to offer ideas about possible types of scholarship that could be helpful for doctoral students and junior scholars. Every decision about scholarship is political. It signals our choices about how we want to intervene in public. Choices are explicit or implicit responses to the question "What can we do with communication studies?" To mention a few options: spread civic knowledge; help people cope with personal and social challenges; foster citizenship and democratic communication practices; empower people; offer tools to live healthier lives; help organizations make better decisions and be more inclusive; give visibility to silenced voices; stimulate critical consciousness; and tackle a host of social problems – from loneliness to inequality.

Positions and decisions about public scholarship are entangled with a host of critical issues: the purpose and the politics of scholarship; university expectations, opportunities, and rewards; academic careers; academic cultures; life trajectories and personal/professional identities; situational politics; and citizenship commitments and conditions. These issues inevitably shape our decisions about who we want to be as scholars and why we produce knowledge. They underpin the way we resolve multiple considerations, including expectations, constraints, incentives, opportunities, risks, and perceptions. In the end, how we deftly navigate academic life shapes the kind of (public) scholar we want to be.

With this question in mind, I examine a range of public interventions by communication scholars in different settings and areas of expertise. I do not intend to offer a comprehensive survey of the global landscape of communication studies – a virtually impossible task. Instead, my goals are more modest: to rethink contemporary forms of public scholarship (Chapter 1); to examine the purpose (Chapter 2), positions (Chapter 3), and practices (Chapter 4) of public scholarship by considering selected examples; and to submit proposals for action (Chapter 5), with the hope that they could serve as a springboard for conversations, reflection, and interventions.

1

Public Scholarship

What is public scholarship?

When I mentioned I was writing a book about public scholarship in communication studies, colleagues responded with a volley of concepts: action-oriented, action research, activist, advocacy, applied, committed, community-based, engaged, political scholarship, and public intellectualism. They were not wrong. Those concepts indicate various forms of public interventions, actions, and principles. They make a conceptual alphabet soup that refers to public scholarship. Public scholarship, however, is broader than those concepts. It is an umbrella term that covers scholars' engagement with publics beyond academia.

Cleaning up conceptual brushes will help to clarify the meaning of public scholarship.

Public scholarship may be activist (Frey & Palmer, 2017) or advocacy depending on the motivations and the positions chosen by individual scholars or demanded by non-academic actors and partners, a topic to which I return below. Both concepts refer to taking specific, normative positions vis-à-vis any possible public issue: from improving digital access to strengthening news literacy skills. Yet not all public scholarship necessarily takes open normative positions in favor of certain ideals. Scholars also participate in the public sphere as scientific experts and accomplished practitioners who do not take open political stands on public issues. They passionately stick to their calling and expertise: designing surveys, reporting stories, creating storyboards, teaching code, leaving personal politics out.

Public scholarship can be "committed" and "community-oriented," but the meaning of these concepts is not immediately clear. Scholars can be "committed" to various causes and principles – from science to socialism – even within the confines of academic scholarship. Likewise, scholarship can be oriented to different types of communities defined by geography, race, belief, practice, and so on. Community, a perennially ambivalent concept and normative ideal, can be virtuous or toxic, democratic or authoritarian. You may seek refuge in communities or run away from them.

Public scholarship can be "action research" and "applied" forms of knowledge, but it is not necessarily so. Communication scholars may intervene in other capacities that do not always involve research or applied competencies in the conventional senses. They also participate in various roles: trainers, advisors, strategists, community mobilizers, and so on.

Political scholarship is close to public scholarship, in the sense that the word "political," as Roland Barthes (1972, pp. 172–173) put it, describes "the whole of human relations in their real, social structure, in their power of making the world." Understood as denominating the realm of the public, "political" is another name for public scholarship, without necessarily being strictly partisan or allied with specific social forces. Also, one could reasonably argue that any type of scholarship is political because it implicitly or deliberately implies taking a position in the world about questions and problems, the purpose and the uses of knowledge, and the linkages between scholarly production and society.

Public intellectualism and its problems

"Public intellectual/ism," a concept with a rich tradition in the history of ideas and the sociology of intellectuals, deserves lengthier attention for it has been the most common name for "public scholarship." Public intellectuals are, in Russell Jacoby's (1987, p. 5) definition, "writers and thinkers who address a general and educated audience." On both sides of the North Atlantic, the Mount Rushmore of public intellectuals of the past half-century features a list of (mostly male and white) luminaries. An incomplete, arbitrary list includes Isaiah Berlin, Allan Bloom, Judith Butler, Manuel Castells, Noam Chomsky, Ta Nehisi Coates, Richard Dawkins, Michael Eric Dyson, Niall Ferguson, Henry Louis Gates, Jr., Anthony Giddens, Germaine Greer, Stuart Hall, Bernard Henri-Lévy, Naomi Klein, Paul Krugman, Marshall McLuhan, Steven Pinker, Bertrand Russell, Jeffrey Sachs, Edward Said, Jean-Paul Sartre, Susan Sontag, Cass Sunstein, Cornel West, Howard Zinn, and Slavoj Žižek.

Certainly, those in this motley crew of names have no obvious commonalities, other than being well-known people, with recognizable public presence as (mostly media) commentators on important issues of the day, and identified with various political, social, and cultural causes. "Public intellectuals" are individuals with academic credentials and/or positions who have a regular presence in the public, primarily in the news media as interviewees, op-ed contributors, and sources of news quotes. Some occasionally make movie cameos and feature in documentaries, and most regularly give presentations on lecture circuits and at book fairs. Some rub elbows with political and economic elites, with whom they interact in different capacities, and join in high-profile panels and meetings. Others are stellar figures of ideological positions, contemporary science, public campaigns, government policies, and so on. Some are well-known dissidents or spokespersons identified with struggles against various forms of discrimination and oppression. They rub against the establishment: they are present-day incarnations of the intellectual *maudit* who exercises the right to use public reason against power. Many are known for speaking about their own particular academic expertise in a given field as well as a broad range of contemporary issues: nuclear politics, geopolitics, cultural crisis, development, globalization, war and conflict, nationalism.

Public intellectualism is different from public scholarship. It does not capture the multifaceted forms in which academics engage with publics. It is embedded in outdated and limited notions of publicity that do not capture multiple actions and sites in the public sphere, and the places of ideas in contemporary societies. The notion of "public" in "public intellectual" is tied to the old media order: a hierarchical, pyramidal structure which a few intellectuals could access to share their expertise and views about the world. Public intellectualism is basically mediated presence. It is grounded in a time when mass publicity basically meant media presence. As the central gatekeeper of public life, "the media" determined which ideas and intellectuals were public. Because the public was assimilated to "media publics," public intellectuals were individuals who regularly appeared on the media (Posner, 2002). This order has collapsed largely owing to the unprecedented changes brought about by the digital revolution, namely the proliferation of public platforms and new forms of communication and information flows and action.

Another problem is that "public intellectual" is loaded with assumptions about a specific kind of publicity: media appearances. However, even if massive publicity in contemporary societies remains strongly tied to media presence, appearances in legacy news and digital platforms are only one manifestation of public scholarship. We shouldn't make public intellectualism synonymous with media appearances. Even if "deep mediatization" (Couldry & Hepp, 2016) is a defining feature of contemporary societies, plenty of public scholarship takes place beyond the media. Communication scholars engage in public scholarship even if they do not have a prominent presence in the mainstream media, are go-to names for festival organizers, fill lecture halls, offer wisdom on public matters, or work with political actors: elites, think tanks, activists, or insurgents. Just as there is no media-centric public, publicity, and public sphere anymore (if there ever was), media-centric public intellectualism is inadequate to capture the multiple forms and spaces of public scholarship.

Another problem is that public intellectualism endorses a limited form of knowledge and competencies. It is attached to the value of the written word and the ability to articulate positions verbally in front of large audiences. Jean-Paul Sartre, an emblematic example of twentieth-century public intellectualism in the West, defined it as the politically committed writer turning words into actions. Public intellectuals possess admirable written and verbal skills (and charisma, in some cases) that make their media presence appealing, captivating, and/or popular. Furthermore, they reflect the celebrification of public knowledge, the star system of the public dissemination of ideas: a top-down system of idea production based on individual rather than collective forms of knowledge sharing.

In summary, the notion of public intellectualism is fraught with analytical and normative problems: it is outdated at a time of profound redefinition of the media and the public sphere; it is narrowly associated with skills dear to traditional scholarship; and it is premised on an individual-centered, hierarchical model of knowledge production and dissemination.

Public scholarship as public connections

So what is public scholarship? Aren't essential acts of scholarship, such as teaching, writing, and, obviously, publishing, ways to make knowledge public? Isn't all scholarship public insofar as it takes place in public arenas: classrooms, journals, conferences?

Understanding public scholarship requires clarifying the meaning of "public": a central yet perennially ambiguous concept for communication studies and other fields of inquiry in the social sciences and the humanities. No single definition adequately captures the multiple approaches to the study of "public." Library shelves are packed with literature that discusses "public" and adjacent concepts: publicity, public sphere, the public, public space, public media.

Although I cannot do justice to this rich and open debate within the space of this book, here I identify "public" with connecting individuals, institutions, and ideas. To make public is to connect with others, as Hannah Arendt (1958) argued. Public is the essence of the social, a way to foster social bonds and recognition with and by others; it is the construction of different communities. To make public means to make visible: to enlarge the sphere of action, to make issues common, to expose ideas to others. In contrast, privacy is about disconnection: being left alone, withdrawing into personal spaces, shutting others off, limiting the possibilities for external view and scrutiny. Being private means to be protected from intrusive, external gaze: to reduce, curb, and shut off engagement with the public.

From this perspective, I define public scholarship as the engagement of scholars with non-academic publics. It entails the diversification of knowledge and the amplification of the reach of intellectual production. It raises the visibility of ideas and produces different forms of knowledge that do not always fit conventional academic requirements: scientific rigor, theoretical grounding, data-driven, original contributions to the state of the art. It results in increased exposure of various forms of expression among various publics. Whereas scholarship is primarily concerned with making knowledge public among scholars, public scholarship is making ideas public among myriad publics.

Just like public life, public scholarship builds connections with and through institutions: the spaces where ideas become public. Theorists of public life (Habermas, 1989) and public communication (Garnham, 1990) have underscored the significance of the institutional architecture that sustains "the public." The abstract idea of the public comes into existence in specific spaces: eighteenth-century coffeehouses and salons, nineteenth-century newspapers and union halls, twentieth-century public squares and broadcasts, and twenty-first-century social media. Just as publics congregate in physical and virtual spaces, spaces bring publics into existence. They are sites for establishing and cultivating connections. They build publics defined by legal status, nationality, market position, social markers, collective identities.

Scholarship and public scholarship operate in different institutional spheres. Scholarship primarily takes place in academic institutions: universities, professional associations, journals, books. Although it also takes places in virtual networks set up for research and teaching collaboration and exchange, belonging to universities and counting on a functional institutional infrastructure are fundamental aspects of academic life. Scholarship suffers when external forces, such as commercial imperatives, legal restrictions, and political pressures, unduly influence academic institutions.

In contrast, public scholarship requires expanding the institutional scope and the publics of academic work. It demands establishing connections with myriad institutions: the media, political parties, government agencies, international bodies, non-governmental organizations (NGOs), activists' groups. "Going public" refers to taking one's work beyond academic spaces by making ideas, findings, and expertise visible among various publics in different sites. Doing public scholarship entails different ways of engaging with publics. It demands going beyond the traditional publics of academic work: colleagues, students, manuscript and proposal reviewers, editors (as well as dear loved ones who listen to us with unpredictable, uneven levels of interest). It also includes bringing publics into academic spaces to discuss common interests and produce relevant knowledge with practical implications.*

Public scholarship is as multifaceted as the public and public spaces. It takes place in many spaces in the institutional infrastructure of the public sphere: community associations, unions, media collectives, media, NGOs, government agencies, research institutions, foundations, schools. It is generally a collective enterprise that involves working with other actors and institutions to pursue common goals. It comprises disaggregated forms and spaces in the public sphere. Scholars build different kinds of connections with publics depending on personal skills and competencies as well as institutional opportunities. There is no single path to go public given multiple options: actors, spaces, and goals.

Public scholarship demands skills beyond writing and speaking, which are central to academic scholarship. Communication researchers who work with various publics have many abilities: writing scripts; shooting, producing, and editing video; providing counsel; moderating conversations; collecting and analyzing data; developing curricula and teaching;

* I am indebted to Patria Román-Velázquez for raising this issue during our conversations.

fund-raising; offering recommendations. They inform, advocate, educate, discuss ideas, learn, lend expertise, agitate, criticize, and share their research and views. They participate in several roles: researchers, expert witnesses, translators, trainers, facilitators.

Public scholarship foregrounds collective, participatory forms of knowledge production and sharing. It is not narrowly identified with scholars who impart knowledge. Instead, scholars collaborate with multiple actors around specific problems and solutions. There is no single blueprint, set of competencies, and set of expectations in the way one thinks about specific forms of public scholarship, such as "action research" and "committed."

Public scholarship is inspired by myriad political, ideological, and ethical premises and objectives. It should not be narrowly identified with particular goals or ideological positions. Public scholarship may foster democracy by building communities of practice and knowledge, bring out voices, and activate citizenship. It is linked to a range of political and civic organizations: unions, churches, communities, political parties, social movements. It works to support the goals of government agencies to pursue the public good or particular interests. It partners with international agencies in support of human rights: legal, social, civic. It is driven to gain public recognition and bolster individual presence.

In sum, public scholarship takes different forms. It makes connections with publics in society. It seeks publicity for different reasons: to bring issues to public attention, to persuade policy-makers and citizens, to conduct situation diagnosis, to identity solutions to social problems, to promote social change, and to spread ideas.

2

Purpose

The purpose of academic scholarship is seemingly clear, at least for scholars. We produce knowledge to test theories and arguments, to add novel insights to a body of intellectual work, to educate students, to inform teaching with fresh studies, to upend conventional wisdom, to understand real-world problems better.

In contrast, the goal of public scholarship is less obvious. There are many reasons why scholars choose to be active outside academe.

Public scholarship can be inspired by the desire to do good with and for others – to make personal contributions to society. It is driven by the will to champion issues that are personally relevant, to leave public testimony of ideas and sentiments unconstrained by the conventions of academic publishing, to spread the reach of one's work, and to maximize opportunities for public expression.

Moreover, partnerships with governments and the private sector may bring research funding opportunities to scholars and universities.

In many countries, public scholarship is a common strategy out of necessity to bring in supplemental income. Labor precarity and meager pay push scholars to seek additional sources of income from consulting, teaching, and advising governments, unions, media companies, NGOs, and the private sector, while they hold university positions.

Public scholarship is also driven by self-promotion: personal interest in boosting one's reputation. It is a narcissistic act to build and maintain public recognition, a rather popular and sought-after commodity at this time of the "promotional intellectual" (Williams, 2018). Building a personal, public brand is common and even encouraged by universities, publishers, friends, and peer pressure. Academics are certainly not immune to the politics of branding in the promotional society (Marwick, 2013).

Rarely does a single reason drive public scholarship. Just as pure egoism and the hope of improving society inspire writing, as George Orwell (1968) dryly observed in his classic essay "Why I Write," the motivation to engage with non-academic publics may be either prosaic or altruistic. Public scholarship might be inspired by myriad reasons: curiosity about knotty communication and social problems; identification with the plight of one's in-group; empathy and solidarity with out-groups; self-advancement; self-admiration; cosmopolitan consciousness; broad ethical, religious, and/or political commitments.

Regardless of the driving factor – from healthy narcissism to indefatigable commitment to citizens in need – public scholarship should contribute to making societies more humane, egalitarian, democratic, tolerant, rational, other-oriented, and emphatic.

Public scholarship in communication studies needs to help address two sets of challenges in contemporary societies: communication problems such as misinformation, prejudice, hatred, and exclusivist identities that undermine democratic societies grounded in tolerance, solidarity, and social justice; and the communication dimensions of a host of social problems that result from the politics of exploitation, greed, violence, and exclusion. Confronting both communication and social problems is particularly urgent amid troubling conditions in contemporary societies.

What communication problems? Here I understand communication broadly, as a post-discipline that comprises various areas of expertise in the areas of information, persuasion, dialogue, and sense-making at multiple levels: from the individual to the system (Waisbord, 2019). A comprehensive, catholic notion of communication is grounded in the ubiquity of communication processes and the impossibility of understanding social life without communication. To paraphrase Ludwig Wittgenstein's idea of culture: communication is just there; it's what we do.

We are currently experiencing a multifaceted backlash against decades-long advances in the global expansion of the human rights of groups identified by gender, sexuality, race, ethnicity, political views, religion, and legal condition. It is undeniable that important, uneven advances were made in the past half-century, particularly in the legal recognition of human rights, even if concrete actions fell short and structural inequalities widened. Yet peddlers of fear, hate, and ignorance have shrewdly exploited social divides, anxieties, and narrow-mindedness to mobilize against rights-based policies and movements pushing for social equality and legal recognition. They have injected new energies into the multiple facets of political reaction: nationalism, xenophobia, racism, homophobia, misogyny.

Public scholarship connects communication

scholars with publics in their efforts to understand and resolve communication and social problems.

The challenges of public communication

Public communication in contemporary societies suffers from numerous problems.

When multiple interests and identities are broken up, scattered, pushed away from each other, societies exhibit troubling communication fractures in expressions of incivility, intolerance, prejudice, and misplaced fears. Communication rifts breed the politics of exclusion, hatred, and distrust, which are contrary to democratic, collective understanding and reasoning.

Public communication is endangered when censorship, in its multiple forms, suppresses dissident voices – when powerful actors and ordinary citizens team up to harass, persecute, stigmatize, and silence others. Suppressing the expression of others contradicts fundamental rights and deprives everyone of the opportunity to listen to different, inconvenient opinions.

Public communication is threatened when propaganda and dis/misinformation are pervasive – when governments allied with corporations deliberately misinform citizens to perpetuate elites in power, to disguise the real motivations of rulers, and to trick citizens into believing fictions. Propaganda has taken a different shape lately as ordinary citizens willingly participate in daily, elaborate disinformation campaigns or unwillingly reproduce absolute falsehoods.

Public communication suffers when demagogues continually spread a toxic rhetoric of lies, exaggerations, and falsehood, repeated by media acolytes who march in lockstep with actual and potential dictators. Public communication suffers when crowds believe demagogues who use self-serving lies and platitudes to weaponize the crooked timber of humanity, and who are vehemently hostile to citizens and institutions driven to check, criticize, and hold power accountable.

Public communication is limited when media and industrial corporations wield uncontrolled power over offline and online environments. They make decisions that affect the opportunities for citizens to express their ideas, have access to information, protect their privacy, engage with others at the expense of basic human rights: knowledge, privacy, transparency. Furthermore, digital life has deepened past communication problems as anti-democratic actors find new ways to perpetuate intolerance, misinformation, falsehoods, and power abuses. Moreover, as well as providing plentiful opportunities for bullying, harassment, surveillance, and invasion of privacy, it has generated novel forms of anti-social behavior such as trolling and doxing.

These problems of public communication have become defining features of contemporary digital societies. Some problems involve large, powerful actors engaging in anti-democratic behavior. The consequences of the unbounded power of states and corporations are apparent. Governments have colluded with corporations to monitor citizens and to violate individual privacy. Internet giants such as Facebook and Google exercise arbitrary, unaccountable censorship of content and cozy up to authoritarian governments to further corporate goals devoid of any relevance to democracy or respect for fundamental human rights.

Thus, three decades into the revolution brought about by the World Wide Web, it is undeniable that the digital society has not magically solved long-standing communication problems, as many boldly predicted. In fact, it has brought in new challenges to public life and exacerbated old ones. Rosy social forecasts concocted by Silicon Valley and its allies during the early days of the Internet now sound hollow and self-serving. Their enthusiastic visions of a global Shangri-La made possible by digitalization have fallen flat in the face of the dark corners of digital life. Communication technology is not necessarily the solution to communication problems. Try reading Mark Zuckerberg's 2017 "Bringing the World Closer Together" post without laughing aloud, frowning, or spitting out your coffee.

The corporate rhetorical sleight-of-hand of appropriating the mantle of freedom, creativity, and global community is apparent. Governments have been accessories to the phenomenal expansion of digital giants at the expense of the defense of democratic values: transparency, privacy, public inquiry. Sure, astute observers already knew that ahistorical and self-interested interpretations of the liberating powers of information technology were just corporate pap, thinly disguised as self-assured forecasts of a better future, and massively supported by deep advertising pockets. As the true workings of Internet giants have been exposed by a series of scandals, the mendacity of corporate techno-optimism is now, however, plainly evident. Business models organized around routine, systematic violations of privacy and fostering traffic are not quite the messianic harbingers of radiant news that we were promised.

Altogether, these communication problems amount to a formidable list of challenges for public life. Given the complexity and the magnitude of the communication problems for public life, communication studies has much to contribute to help the public understand and act, individually and collectively. Regardless of the specific issue under scrutiny, communication scholarship should document problems, explain why they are important, and sketch out and test alternatives. The guiding principle needs to be the promotion of democratic communication grounded in public ethics. It needs to foreground dialogue across difference, fact-based collective reasoning, empathy, tolerance, repressed voices, and inclusivity. Finding ways to make accumulated knowledge and interests relevant to society at large is imperative.

How have communication scholars contributed to addressing the current challenges of public communication?

Scholars have joined activists and policy-makers in support of reforms of media and cultural environments to overturn policies that favor narrow government and corporate interests. They have collaborated to bolster media pluralism in the form of alternative, community, non-profit, and public media (Segura & Waisbord, 2016). They have advocated for policy reforms aimed at strengthening public issues and ethics: supporting Internet neutrality; sponsoring free software; bringing quality Internet access to specific communities; limiting media property and diversifying funding to bolster media diversity; strengthening labor laws protecting media workers; supporting adequate funding for public broadcasting (Canella, 2016; J. A. Smith, Lloyd & Pickard, 2015). To support these goals, scholars have lent their expertise in multiple ways. They have provided expert testimony in legislative bodies, produced policy briefs, conducted research, presented findings, made recommendations, participated in advocacy activities, and developed ideas for media policy literacy (Ali & Herzog, 2018; Lentz, 2014a, 2014b).

Communication scholars have also partnered with communities in the development of initiatives to support local media and local storytelling (Wright 2018), to stimulate civic engagement (Son & Ball-Rokeach, 2016), and to improve health conditions (Wilkin, 2013). Scholars have also collaborated with media producers and policy-makers to promote socially oriented content in the media. They have studied social inequalities in media representation and pushed to increase the presence of under-represented groups (S. L. Smith, Choueiti & Pieper, 2016). They have collaborated in the development and the production of news content, film and television scripts, documentaries, video games, and radio programs.

A growing area of public scholarship are initiatives that bring together scholars with journalists and news organizations. They have collaborated on several activities, such as documenting the state of the news industry, fostering innovate forms of reporting, conducting research of funding models and news use, and supporting the development of specific reporting competencies (Napoli, Stonbely, McCollough & Renninger, 2017). Scholars have also worked with news organizations to develop content that promotes civic behaviors and attitudes (Stroud, 2017). In the United States, several programs have been established in recent years, such as the Center for Media Engagement at the University of Texas, the Center for Cooperative Media at Montclair State University, and the News Co/Lab at Arizona State University. These initiatives generally take place in research-practice laboratories that tackle specific, concrete problems affecting journalism and the news industry. These initiatives aim to bridge gaps between academia and newsrooms by providing spaces for study and reflection on common subjects of interest. These initiatives take partnerships beyond the traditional forms of participation by individual scholars as trainers and lecturers in journalism workshops.

Media literacy has been another important, fruitful area of intervention to address many of the challenges previously mentioned, especially with young citizens. Scholars have collaborated with governments, foundations, and NGOs in the development and implementation of programs by conducting research, developing curricula in schools, providing recommendations for implementation, and conducting program assessments (Eckert, Metzger-Riftkin & Nurmis, 2018; Livingstone et al., 2017).

Global social problems and communication

Public scholarship in communication studies is also central for addressing myriad global social problems: social inequality, wealth concentration, war and conflict, disease, climate change, pollution, racism, misogyny, xenophobia, political persecution, sexual discrimination, forced migration, homophobia, labor exploitation, and slavery.

Undoubtedly, these problems are not simply caused by multiple social forces: turbo-charged capitalism, social hatred, nationalism, corporate greed, exploitation, and political power. However,

they are also perpetuated by communication processes. Propaganda keeps problems invisible and/
or misunderstood, contributes to deflecting responsibilities and blaming the wrong factors and actors,
and leads to misguided decisions and solutions.
Misinformation among elites and ordinary citizens
causes anti-social actions and ill-judged policies.
The lack of public awareness accounts for the invisibility of social problems in the public sphere, social
ignorance, and forgetfulness.

Just as they are part of the problem, communication actions are central to redressing social inequality,
improving social conditions, and promoting more
humane social relationships. Information helps to
increase awareness about social problems through
news coverage, media storytelling, and advocacy.
Participation and deliberation are critical to assess
causes and debate positive actions, especially
in communities confronting poverty and social
exclusion (Collier & Lawless, 2016). Videos and
documentaries have been extensively used to spark
critical reflexivity and activism (Robé, Wolfson &
Funke, 2016). Media messaging and interpersonal
communication in small groups, families, and communities foster social behaviors as well as empathy
and solidarity. Communication actions have a vital
role to play in breaking the silence and ending the

invisibility, expressing views and demands, discussing causes, figuring out solutions, and moving to action.

Communication scholars have utilized their expertise in their work with various non-academic institutions and publics to collaborate in a range of interventions to address these problems.

Health communication scholars often collaborate with governments, NGOs, international agencies, donors, and public–private partnerships to achieve several goals: inform citizens about healthy choices; foster community participation to address social inequities; raise awareness about health problems and inequalities; destigmatize diseases and affected people; advocate for better health services and health policy reforms that result in more equitable allocation of funding and other resources. Areas of interventions include prominent issues in global public health such as tobacco control, infectious diseases, maternal and child health, eating disorders, cardiovascular diseases, cancer, and many others.

Likewise, scholars interested in communication for development and social change have long collaborated with international organizations, including technical agencies, donors, NGOs, and activists' associations. Their work covers a wide range of issues: rural development, poverty reduction, children's education and empowerment, women's rights, health and wellbeing, environmental sustainability, economic development, gender roles, and employment. Specific contributions show the enormous variety of communication actions used to promote social justice: communication technologies and interpersonal skills to document local problems and views; awareness-raising actions among policymakers, opinion leaders, and citizens; community journalism and storytelling to raise consciousness; community mobilization to develop critical thinking and action (Kolucki & Lemish, 2011); improving digital access to build life skills among young citizens (Livingstone et al., 2017); collaborating with media organizations to strengthen the quality of news coverage of social problems; advocating for environment rights in ecologies damaged by extractivist industries (Palma, 2015); promoting social behaviors through positive messages embedded in entertainment content; and promoting debates in post-conflict settings to spur dialogue, peace, and integration.

Communication scholars have also worked on actions to improve opportunities for and conditions of socially marginalized populations. Scholars have developed partnerships with immigrant communities to bolster urban regeneration by using a panoply of research and practical methodologies to stimulate participation, seek partnerships, influence policies, and assess impact (Román-Velázquez, 2014; Villanueva et al., 2017). Others have collaborated with donors and communities to reduce digital inequality among low-income families by developing grounded views of media policies informed by surveys and engaging with policy-makers (Katz & Gonzalez, 2016).

Shifting perspectives

In summary, a wealth of experiences suggest that public scholarship contributes to addressing current communication problems at the core of contemporary societies. Communication interventions help to connect groups across differences; promote dialogue in interpersonal and group settings; bolster the expression of a range of views in society in large- and small-scale environments; address the information needs of communities; denounce insidious forms of misinformation; persuade various publics to attend to social problems and to embrace pro-social attitudes and behaviors; and educate and empower publics in media engagement.

To turn the social potential of communication

studies into concrete actions, we need to reorient the gravitational center of intellectual work: shift the perspective from producing knowledge for fellow scholars to also developing competencies and expertise to engage with multiple publics.

Certainly, we make our work public when we publish, present ideas in professional meetings, and lead classroom discussions. As members of academic communities, we constantly engage with many publics. However, we primarily write, teach, and speak for other academics, students, friends, colleagues. This is what the institutional design of academe is structured to promote – academic scholarship according to specific standards of excellence: rigorously researched, theoretically learned and sophisticated, methodologically sound, intellectually creative.

Communication scholarship, like any form of professionalization, entails separation from the language, thinking, and perspective of ordinary life. No wonder we tend to live in rarefied environments. The way we write and talk leads to insularity. We (proudly) use inscrutable prose. One must be esoteric to get respect and recognition from fellow jargon-speakers, a characteristic that many observers bemoan for it distances scholars from society (Kristof, 2014).

Purpose

What's wrong with only working in the rarefied environments of universities? Being removed from society is a logical outgrowth of the process of academic professionalization, but the consequence is that publics rarely learn or benefit from the accumulation of knowledge – the rich trove of ideas we produce. At a time of widespread questions about the contributions of scholarly expertise, negative views about universities, and doubts about the scientific enterprise, this should not be simply seen as a failure to "communicate" with others, or just as a curious feature of academic scholarship – so relevant to a few, so unknown to many.

Making public scholarship is one way of asserting the social relevance of communication studies in the face of the furious anti-science, anti-rights crusade that right-wing populism launched just as postmodernism was about to hammer the last nail in the coffin of the scientific paradigm. Over time, these reactionary fanatics have eroded the credibility of science, hollowed out universities and scientific agencies, and rebutted fact-based policy recommendations.

The popularity and political might of counter-scientific, anti-human rights positions is reflected in rising skepticism about climate change, immunization, and medical treatments, and growing denialism of genocide. Such views are now common in the mainstream. They are not marginal, wild, flat-earth views orbiting in a different social sphere. Rather, they are easily available on social media. They are regularly expressed by prominent public officials and powerful institutions who endorse ideas that defy basic scientific conclusions as well as values that contradict fundamental international human rights legislation.

These are not simply dangerous alternatives that reasonably challenge the universalist premises of the scientific paradigm. Nor do they defend alternative forms of knowledge in the name of pluralism and democracy, listening and understanding. Nor do they champion relativism as a healthy, necessary corrective to scientific objectivity. Rather, they question the entire academic enterprise, regardless of its multiple paradigms: positivist, critical, structural. In return they offer knowledge grounded in convictions and dogma rather than facticity and rigor.

The ignorance about the accumulated knowledge in communication studies among the public is also troubling. Even people who should be our natural interlocutors (e.g. media practitioners, community organizers, policy-makers, technical/policy experts) find us too abstract, too theoretical, too removed from everyday concerns. This is especially worrisome for many of us who tackle real-world problems in our research and hope to produce socially relevant knowledge. If we were just dedicated to esoteric pursuits, detached from concrete matters that preoccupy citizens, then it wouldn't be so surprising or alarming that neither "the public" nor "experts" understand us. Yet many of us study actual social problems that impact people's lives, such as misinformation, anti-social uses of digital technology, the risks of media use, negative media representations, information inequality, and so on.

Undoubtedly, engaging with non-academic publics is a risky proposition. It threatens perceptions of the value of our work, reputation, credibility – what we tirelessly, patiently, and passionately build over years. We may command strong respect from other scholars, but be completely unknown or misunderstood by non-academic publics because we don't talk their language or are concerned with purely academic pursuits.

In search of mutual understanding, we should be translators and brokers, positioned between academic and non-academic worlds. We should be cognizant of priorities and needs among various publics. We should hope to be accessible: to develop a clear prose (or speak the local language), simplify complex ideas, condense labyrinthine literatures into a few sentences in the vernacular, provide straightforward suggestions and answers, make ideas relevant to public concerns. Public engagement demands finding common ground with others – most notably, in the language we use, the ideas we discuss, and the purpose of knowledge. We also need to understand why specific publics want to collaborate with us: what they want to achieve, how they perceive us, what they think we can help with. In turn we may bring specific skills, contacts, legitimacy, opportunities, experience.

We need to capitalize on the reservoir of a wealth of knowledge, evidence, and arguments in communication studies to make contributions to public life. As communication scholars, we have much to contribute if we reorient our work from writing for academics to engaging with various publics. This shift demands stepping outside our comfort zones, the wonderful cocoon of academic life, in order to figure out how to make ideas practical and relevant. By shifting the perspective, we also benefit from the reciprocal nature of public scholarship.* Just as publics benefit from our contributions, we also learn from publics. It is not only about what scholars can give the public; it is also about what we

---

* I thank Dafna Lemish for bringing up this point in our conversation.

learn from publics in ways that make our scholarship and interventions more attuned to public needs and demands, rather than being oriented exclusively around academic priorities and research directions.

We owe this shift in the purpose of scholarship to the public that supports academic work through taxes and tuition fees, backs funding and policies for higher education, and trusts us with educating students. We owe to the publics we study – it is a way of giving back to the people who give us their insights, trust, knowledge. We owe it to ourselves – to be reminded why our work should matter beyond academic knowledge, and why our expertise and insights can make a difference in the lives of others. We are uniquely positioned to help societies understand and act upon social problems that are either communicative in nature or grounded in communication processes.

3

Practice

Motivations

Why practice public scholarship? What motivates scholars to do so? Isn't scholarship a sufficient contribution to the public good? Isn't the production of knowledge about important communication issues enough contribution to society?

Undoubtedly, research, teaching, and service are public-oriented actions. They connect scholars with others: students, colleagues, funders, and occasionally the reading public. Yet public scholarship is inspired by the belief that academic scholarship is limited. As fulfilling and important as it is, academic life does not fully capture the production and sharing of knowledge. Nor does it exhaust the ways scholars may contribute to society.

45

Public scholarship is not something that universities generally expect, stimulate, or reward. Generally, it is neither promoted and cultivated by graduate programs nor considered a fundamental part of scholarship and academic careers. As leading universities prioritize, support, and reward "scholarship for scholars," public scholarship is generally the outgrowth of personal desires and convictions, and so understanding these personal motivations is important.

The drive to practice public scholarship reflects the notion that intellectual work overflows conventional academic boundaries. Public scholarship is grounded in a normative vision about the necessity to engage with non-academic publics. Three beliefs inspire this work: the intertwined nature of scholarly and applied work in various areas of communication studies; the value of knowledge produced by non-academic actors; and the nature of scholarship as a political act that transcends academic campuses.

Public scholarship as applied work

Although numbers are hard to come by, it is not unusual for many communication researchers to have a background in other occupations and sectors. Before they became researchers, they were practitioners in various areas that are part of communication studies: journalism, broadcasting, filmmaking, international development, education and training, activism, public relations, public health, government, and international and social development. Therefore, for them, public scholarship is the continuation of work they did before becoming full-time scholars. It reflects the double orientation of scholars whose work is grounded in academia and other institutions. Working with non-academic actors is not something separate from research, but rather it is another facet of the work. Academic and public scholarship are two sides of the same endeavor. They nurture each other: just as scholarship provides ideas to guide practice, practical interventions help generate ideas and infuse research and teaching.

Scholars with backgrounds in applied communication work generally have contacts with and institutional knowledge of non-academic institutions and publics. These competencies are critical for developing and maintaining contacts, as well as for understanding what partners and communities expect and how they may benefit from their participation. Applied work demands a range of skills that are not generally taught in doctoral programs primarily geared to train future researchers. It also demands an appreciation of practitioners' jargon, organizational priorities, and contextual expectations of where journalists, policy-makers, teachers, activists, funders, and other actors work. Without a solid understanding of how partners work, public scholarship is unlikely to be taken seriously in terms of offering something important, unique, and relevant. Likewise, a knowledge of contexts of practice helps with the evaluation of points of entry, strategic opportunities, and results.

The idea of public scholarship as applied work is also guided by the sense that opportunities and achievements outside academia may be as rewarding and significant as traditional academic work, and that getting recognition from communities, journalists, and ordinary citizens is as important as acknowledgment from academic peers. Various interventions are extremely rewarding: utilizing video to promote community debates; helping community organizations to raise funding; assisting migrants to navigate complex business and legal issues; discussing documentaries in neighborhood spaces; contributing to messaging in public health campaigns; or training journalists.

Practice

Public scholarship as knowledge production
Undoubtedly, producing academic knowledge has
many benefits. Producing scholarship at a relatively
comfortable distance from society is important for
intellectual freedom and critical thinking, even if
this ideal stands on a precarious balance in many
universities around the world, as political and economic interests undermine academic autonomy.
Scholars who treasure independence and have
worked in universities tightly controlled by partisan
commissars, bean counters, and government hacks
know this well. Minimal levels of institutional
autonomy are necessary to shelter scholars from the
enemies of critical thinking, even if universities exist
in conditions of "complex autonomy" rather than
complete independence from political and economic
powers (Bourdieu, 2008). No academic knowledge
is fully autonomous, and the degrees of autonomy
vary significantly across institutions.

Academic knowledge, however, neither exhausts
nor fully captures all forms of knowledge. To state
the obvious, learning, thinking, and exchanging
ideas take place in public spaces beyond academia:
community centers, governments, schools, health
centers, civic associations, prisons. Knowledge is
produced by all kinds of people, in different forms
and for different reasons. This premise underlies

the work of communication scholars who espouse versions of the notion of situated, local knowledge. Knowledge is an iterative, constant process, embedded in specific communities. Knowledge is experiential: it is not only library work, experimental research, or surveys. Knowledge is not guarded behind academic walls. It is open and public in ways that unsettle conventional definitions of "the knowledgeable" and "the known" subjects: the actors who actively know.

Academic scholarship should reflect myriad forms of knowledge. It needs to make people's stories public and elevate the presence of popular knowledge in academia. Communication scholarship brings up histories, feelings, demands, and insights of people who are often simply seen as "research subjects" or "targets." The conception of community-based knowledge rejects the conventional approach to research which basically views subjects as people from whom data are gathered mainly for the benefit of academics, individually and collectively. Instead, it repositions research: it moves it away from extractivist approaches ("getting data from people") and situates it within local webs of knowledge. It eschews instrumental relationships with "subjects" in favor of research interlaced with local lives. It conceives scholars as facilitators and coordinators rather than separate experts, with limited, impersonal interactions with the "subjects" of study.

This approach to knowledge production underlies public scholarship, which conceptualizes knowledge as an essentially collaborative process with non-academic actors. It is found in interventions that use participatory methods (e.g. critical ethnography, community meetings, grassroots video and theater) to produce knowledge that communities use to understand challenges and needs, to discuss and plan suitable interventions to address specific problems, and to document social conditions and stimulate critical thinking (Basnyat, 2019).

This approach is also manifested in interventions designed to produce knowledge in collaboration with journalists, psychologists, teachers, public health officers, policy-makers, and other actors. Scholars are participants in this process rather than the center of knowledge production. Knowledge is produced to inform decisions about a range of communication issues: media content, media training, media policies, educational curricula, news funding, public health campaigns, internal communication in organizations.

Community-based knowledge production generally takes longer than traditional scholarship.

Establishing partnerships and building trust with communities is not done on the fly. It requires nurturing relationships, defining mutual interests and responsibilities, and identifying expected results and benefits. Personal, frequent contact is necessary. Once initial agreements are settled, every step takes time: identifying common goals, developing protocols, getting university approvals, applying for grants, recruiting participants. When relationships between academic institutions and communities exist, work is easier. Otherwise, scholars need to build relationships, especially if they are not originally from the community or lack personal contacts. Cultivating relationships is especially important in communities that are wary of academic researchers after having seen them come and go in the past – parachuting in to extract information and never heard of again.

Managing expectations takes time, too. Communities may also ask researchers to perform non-research roles such as helping with various tasks – management, fund-raising, training – or helping to connect them with specific networks – whether these are political, groups of donors, or in the private sector. This process is full of uncertainty. What will happen? When? What is needed to start and bring the project to completion? What are the mutually expected outcomes? Considering these particularities, these collaborations entail risk. They demand various steps and time; they include several unknowns that make it necessary to adjust expectations, results, and timelines.

Some collaborations, however, have several advantages. They might yield results faster than conventional academic work. Making studies public and receiving feedback generally take less time than the typical schedule of academic publishing. Work can also reach larger audiences. Knowing that ideas are widely read and inform decision-making processes brings enormous satisfaction: the realization that one's work effectively shapes conversations, thinking, and decisions. This is especially important as a considerable amount of scholarly publishing gets lost amid the growing, staggering volume of academic production.

Public scholarship as politics

The vision of public scholarship as politics also inspires communication scholars to engage with non-academic publics. It embraces the notion that scholarship and politics are intertwined. No firm distinction is drawn between the scholar as "expert" and "public person" committed to issues and causes. It rejects the notion of science as neutral and free from suppositions. Instead, it approaches scholarship as a way of being in the world, informed by personal backgrounds and ethical, religious, and ideological commitments.

Public scholarship can be driven by normative beliefs about "the good society" that undergird several traditions of communication research: communitarian, peace, critical, dialogical, feminist, radical. It taps into theoretical traditions that view communication as community building and dialogue to cultivate "the good society." It positions researchers as public scholars deeply involved in informing and facilitating processes that lead to progressive outcomes. Engaging with publics to raise awareness of common problems is a central charge for researchers, one that holds great promise for fostering democratic, public problem-solving. It is grounded in an approach that treats communication as central to the politics of solidarity and empathy. It is also in keeping with the notion that scholars should contribute to society to pay it back for the manifold forms in which it supports scholarly work.

Public scholarship may also be embedded in personal beliefs and identities. It may be inspired by religious teachings: the Christian call to achieve greatness by helping others to achieve greatness

(Luke 22:25–27), the Jewish concept of *tikkun olam* ("repair the world"), or the Muslim imperative of *islah* ("reform" or "make things better"). Public scholarship may be grounded in secular politics: support for human rights; loyalty to partisan politics and ideologies; identification with demands of specific groups (e.g. workers, refugees, migrants); and commitment to ethics and ideals such as peace promotion, conflict resolution, tolerance, free expression, and citizens' empowerment. Public scholarship may be a way to embrace collective identity – an outgrowth of the sense of belonging to groups articulated by class, gender, race, ethnicity, sexuality, legal status, and language.

In summary, public scholarship reflects personal beliefs about the relationship between research and applied work, the significance of various forms of knowledge production, and the intertwined nature of knowledge and politics.

Context

Personal motivations and individual will are not sufficient to drive public scholarship. Personal visions are not divorced from academic and political contexts. Academics rarely toil in splendid isolation. To paraphrase the classic Marxist dictum, they do not make it as they please, but they work under already existing circumstances. We are not academic Robinson Crusoes free from institutional constraints. Nor are we removed from social conditions that affect scholarly work: politics, economics, cultural backgrounds, intellectual traditions.

Three contextual factors affect the practice of public scholarship: the ambivalent position of universities regarding public scholarship; the pull of academic cultures; and the particularities of national politics.

The ambivalent position of universities

Communication scholars work in universities with specific missions and expectations. Expectations are grounded in particular aspects, such as type of ownership and funding, secular and faith-based mission, research and teaching focus, level of resources, scientific and political traditions, forms of faculty governance, and links to political and corporate actors. These considerations influence institutional demands and expectations as well as views about public scholarship, which are usually under the label of public outreach or public service.

Academic expectations are crystallized in a series of administrative procedures and documents:

annual reviews, peer reviews, tenure and promotion decisions. Scholars at research universities are expected to produce knowledge primarily for fellow academics, who ultimately determine the value of someone's work and merits for particular positions and job security.

Certainly, public scholarship is part of the mission of many universities. For example, land-grant universities in the United States are committed to outreach or service work, frequently invoked by leaders and included in annual reports. Outreach or engaged scholarship is understood as "a scholarly endeavor that cross-cuts teaching, research [and creative activities], and service. It involves generating, transmitting, applying, and preserving knowledge for the direct benefit of external audiences in ways that are consistent with university and unit missions" (The Provost's Committee on University Outreach, 1993). Similar language is found in universities committed to public-facing and public service work around the world. In addition, faith-based universities are institutionally committed to community service grounded in religious precepts. Other universities are supportive of different forms of partnerships, particularly with the private sector: fund-raising, research collaborations, teaching, community outreach.

In recent years, there has been growing interest in and support for public scholarship. Prominent scholars across the disciplines have also defined public scholarship as an obligation, as central to the mission of sociology, political science, anthropology, economics, and others. Universities have supported the creation of programs with the mission to promote public scholarship. The Carnegie Engaged University classification, which recognizes various forms of public scholarship, has become a prestigious, much-coveted distinction.

Despite encouraging signs in selected institutions, research universities continue to favor traditional academic scholarship, and teaching institutions expect scholars to carry heavy classroom loads. Institutional expectations and rewards ensure that scholarly research determines tenure and promotion, praise, and recognition. Public service, often praised by presidents of professional associations and high-level administrators, is hardly a top priority. It is not the main factor affecting employment opportunities and stability. Instead, research universities expect faculty to maintain a steady publication record in academic journals and presses and to have a regular presence in scholarly forums. The push for "professionalization" and excellence, keywords in program evaluations and annual assessments of performance, does not typically emphasize public scholarship.

Institutional expectations tilt academic productivity in favor of the conventional metrics of excellence. Admittedly, this is not new. In his pessimistic account of the state of public intellectualism in the United States, Russell Jacoby (1987) concluded that the politics of tenure overpower other considerations and obligations. In his view, the remarkable expansion of universities in the United States in the 1960s was directly responsible for the erosion of the conditions that nurtured public intellectualism. Amid growing funding, enrollments, and jobs, favorable conditions attracted new crops of scholars to university employment. They needed to conform to administrative demands that were widely different from the free-wheeling atmosphere of urban, bohemian intellectualism of previous decades.* Mid-century public intellectuals embodied a time of café thinkers and street-wise academics who contributed to a string of newspapers, highbrow magazines, and broadcast programs. They wrote for a broad audience and were chiefly interested in holding on to a sense of intellectual purity rather than translating ideas into

---

* Since its publication in 1987, Jacoby's book has sparked much discussion. He has recently reflected on this in *The Chronicle of Higher Education* (Jacoby, 2015).

practice, as Richard Hofstadter (1963) observed in his magisterial analysis of the place of ideas and intellectuals in the United States. Instead, as a long list of scholars argued, from Lewis Coser to Noam Chomsky, the growth of academic jobs as well as the absorption of intellectuals by the welfare state blunted the political edge of scholarly work. David Ricci's (1987) sharp critique of the professionalization of political scientists reflected wide concerns in the disciplines about the limited contributions to society. In his lucid exegesis of twentieth-century French intellectuals, Tony Judt (1992) concluded that the integration of intellectuals into social and political power was contrary to the production of truth.

The professionalization of knowledge resulted in the valuing of productivity of scholarly output over the passion for ideas and criticism, encyclopedic knowledge, and well-rounded training. Leading research universities put enormous value on being a principal investigator and successful fund-raising. The pressure to "publish or perish," especially among junior faculty, trumps other considerations to determine academic merit and performance. Having a regular, strong public presence in different corners of society is not exactly a major consideration.

Although these expectations have long been common in leading universities in the West, they have also become common in preeminent universities around the world in recent times. This is the result of two simultaneous forces: the adoption of neoliberal principles in university administration and management; and the constant pressure to gain international reputation as measured by global rankings.

The neoliberal assault on universities is contrary to public scholarship (Calhoun, 2006). The ascendancy of market-centered principles leads to the adoption of a managerial mindset primarily concerned with improving the bottom line and cutting support for initiatives that are not perceived central to bringing revenues. Public universities have experienced growing demands to demonstrate adequate use of public funds, especially when pro-market governments decide disbursements and evaluations. Deep cuts in research support and faculty positions also push to produce metrics to demonstrate success according to public charters and university missions. As these issues take priority, the corporatization of universities (Washburn, 2005) does not place a great deal of value on work with non-academic publics, unless it brings additional revenues through partnerships with governments and the private sector. Scholarship that does not yield significant gain or represents the underutilization of existing resources is not a priority. Branding is the kind of publicity favored by market-centered universities: activities to build and reaffirm reputation particularly vis-à-vis potential donors and students and their families.

Simultaneously, public and private universities have been in a permanent race to climb up positions in regional and world rankings. The ambition to become globally prestigious is tangible everywhere. Ranking positions have become a common currency that signifies the quality and the prestige of the institution. The information is used by public relations offices to bring global visibility and to attract donors and students.

Both neoliberal policies and the rush to rise in global rankings emphasize metrics that reward academic performance other than public scholarship, such as the volume and the prestige of publications, the size of endowments and research funds, and research and teaching awards. Scholarly metrics are the backbone of external reviews and other forms of evaluation that feed higher education rankings and program assessments. Public scholarship does not fit these conventional metrics that are prioritized to bolster both university revenues and profile.

Even in universities that recognize public outreach, public scholarship doesn't necessarily replace expectations about scholarly output. As universities hold ambivalent and sometimes contradictory views about public engagement (Buckingham, 2013), public scholarship rarely counts much for tenure and promotion. Public scholarship becomes part of the "double shift" of scholarly work: what scholars do in addition to meeting academic expectations.

Universities typically promote and support public scholarship, namely media appearances and high-profile public presentations that bring positive attention and reinforce name recognition and prestige. However, such presence is accepted within certain limits of desirable, approved ideas. Media publicity is praised as long as it is managed within safe ideological boundaries. Less welcome are scholars who take "controversial" positions outside the borders of the mainstream and engage in outspoken critical thinking that attracts negative media storms (Smeltzer & Cantillon, 2015). They bring headaches to upper administration, public relations offices, and influential donors. They generally put universities in a bind: defend free speech vis-à-vis the public outcry generated by faculty statements or cave under pressure (Wilson, 2016).

Power positions in academic settings also affect the practice of public scholarship. To state the obvious, not everyone who holds an academic position enjoys similar power to decide priorities in their careers. This is not just a question of the position particular scholars hold in the academic hierarchy. So, doing public scholarship is ostensibly a courageous act for those with less power whose permanency and prospects depend on assessment from their higher-up colleagues. Power is also inseparable from labor conditions. At a time of widespread and growing labor precarity, public scholarship may be a luxury for many scholars who don't have tenure or job stability. When growing numbers of scholars juggle multiple commitments, public scholarship is a tougher proposition for underpaid and overworked academics. It may not be a priority for junior scholars hoping to secure their jobs by meeting conventional expectations: a steady flow of publications in well-ranked journals and books by recognized publishers, conference presentations, and a successful fund-raising record. Precarious labor conditions are not exactly conducive to public scholarship for it challenges the dominant way of conceptualizing valid knowledge. Furthermore, certain forms of public scholarship, such as community-based knowledge and activist scholarship, are too political and unpredictable, especially when scholars need to deliver tangible results that fit established metrics.

Academic cultures and public scholarship
Managerial principles and the ranking-obsessed mentality are not the only factors responsible for public scholarship's lack of sufficient institutional support. Mainstream academic cultures do not reward it either. Public scholarship is not conventionally seen by peers as central to academic careers, success, and prestige, no matter how frequently administrators and prominent colleagues make passionate calls for academic outreach and public service. In fact, scholars may have rewarding, successful academic careers, with plenty of personal satisfaction and professional recognition, without ever setting a foot outside university campuses. Working with non-academic publics may be detrimental to scholarship. Advisors often warn junior colleagues and doctoral students not to squander academic careers by other distractions. It takes energies away from the essential requirements to secure job stability and get promoted. Public scholarship is not the most direct path to leave a mark in communication studies; to achieve the kind of accomplishments that typically lead to reward: developing trailblazing lines of inquiry, moving the theoretical needle, coining influential concepts, producing original research findings, publishing and not perishing.

The weight of particular academic cultures fosters a distinctive habitus that, although it may be imperative for scholarly success, leads to insularity from society. Insularity is a natural consequence of the fact that academia is the gravitational point of scholarly work. Acceptance by fellow members of particular tribes demands a strong command of that specific academic culture in terms of language, writing, methodological skills, theoretical knowledge and sophistication. Building and cultivating ties to specific communities of scholars demands learning and performing specific professional norms. These dynamics pull scholars into the rarefied environments of academic tribes who are the main audiences, judges, and collaborators – the true influencers of career paths.

Unsurprisingly, scholars who are well equipped to succeed in academia do not necessarily have the skills to engage with other publics, nor do they have the incentive to do so. Overwrought, complex, esoteric language is critical to scholarly success, but it is not the sure path to public scholarship. Even writing for op-ed pages or giving TED Talk presentations demands learning new ways of communicating ideas. Academic jargon is often criticized by potential external partners such as journalists, media producers, filmmakers, and government officials.

They find much of communication scholarship abstract, theoretical, and impenetrable. No wonder we sometimes command as much respect as legal contracts typed in Comic Sans font.

Yet not all academic cultures stand in similar positions vis-à-vis work with non-academic publics. Where the positivist paradigm has a strong grip on communication scholarship, researchers may not be similarly encouraged to work outside academic settings. The exception is the role of scholars as scientific experts. In contrast, academic cultures that do neatly distinguish between scholarship and politics value different forms of work. In Latin America, for example, a long-standing tradition in academia meshes intellectual work with political activism and other forms of intervention in the public sphere (Miller, 1999). The positivist tradition of a clear separation between knowledge and values has not been dominant. Instead, a tradition of progressive, critical scholarship focused on matters related to popular communication and empowerment of socially excluded communities has wielded significant influence (Waisbord, 2014). This tradition has been more amenable to recognizing multiple forms of public engagement beyond academia. Many communication scholars throughout the region, have continued to maintain links to political parties and social movements, particularly on matters related to public communication and policies, and some have held government positions.

Political context

Individual decisions to engage in public scholarship are also shaped by the particularities of the political context. In principle, this matter is relatively simple: the respect for democratic rights guarantees scholarly interventions and partnerships with various actors. In contrast, the shutdown of universities, the censorship and harassment of critical scholars, and violence by state and parastate forces make public scholarship extremely dangerous. In these circumstances, universities are not autonomous spaces for public knowledge and reasoning. Authoritarian politics driven by ethnic, religious, and nationalist ideologies cut off the oxygen needed for free and critical thinking. Authoritarian and semi-authoritarian regimes, as recent cases in Turkey, Hungary, and Singapore demonstrate, have a similar inclination to fire oppositional scholars, close down universities with a reputation for dissent, and suffocate speech. Needless to say, public scholarship is a courageous act under these conditions. It is a form of resistance rather than simply an extension of academic life. Just signing petitions, giving media interviews, having a popular blog or social media account, or publishing critical ideas puts scholars in peril.

However, democracies do not necessarily guarantee ideal conditions for all forms of public scholarship. Some forms of public intervention are audacious acts, too, amid political polarization, the backlash against liberal and progressive views in academia, and the proliferation of digital platforms. The recent ascent of anti-science, anti-intellectual movements make it more likely that certain forms of public expression will be attacked by the current exponents of irrationalism. Large segments of public opinion, particularly on the right, have grown skeptical, if not outright critical, of academics and experts.

So, in this context, positions that cross the boundaries of "legitimate," mainstream discourse or offend dogmatics are more likely to spark public controversy. An incomplete list of positions includes: the condemnation of hate speech in contexts rife with racism and xenophobia; the denunciation of government policies in polarized and violent societies; the denunciation of war-mongering amid turbo-charged jingoism; the criticism of the "deep state" and rogue actors (mafias, drug traffickers) amid lawlessness; the critique of universities with ties to governments and donors identified with anti-democratic positions.

What may be deemed controversial varies according to particular institutional contexts. Denouncing the Catholic Church for abuses may be a dangerous proposition in some countries and universities. Public support for LGBTQ rights is likely to spark different reactions according to whether those rights are legal in a particular country and time in history. Defending the rights of particular peoples (e.g. Palestinians, Kurds, migrants) has different connotations in different national and university settings. Fighting influential corporations with ties to university benefactors and board members may be a risky proposition. Criticizing the politics of war, xenophobia, and racism in the media and other public forums may result in ferocious attacks by right-wing media loudmouths and armies of trolls.

Under these conditions, universities and critical scholars have been targets of pressure, censure, doxing, vicious attacks, even if the formal institutions of democracy exist. The intensity of forces hellbent on asphyxiating critical thinking and free speech, especially on certain "sensitive" issues, widely varies, however, among countries and regions.

Although individual motivations inspire, the practice of public scholarship is intertwined with institutional and political contexts. It is not a purely personal decision. It is shaped by social factors: the commitment of universities, the particularities of academic cultures, and the political environment. Public scholarship, especially if it takes an open and critical bent, is particularly admirable when it is not supported or chastised by administrators, board members, public officials, and the public. Public scholarship is hardly a priority for a managerial mindset that rewards conventional metrics of scholarship and university expectations.

Public scholars need to constantly balance different expectations and pressures. The call by Stine Eckert and Linda Steiner (2018: 234) for fellow feminist communication scholars "to think hard about how to enact their feminist commitments when working simultaneously to satisfy tenure system demands" applies across areas of specialization. Attending to institutional expectations while staying active in non-academic settings and expanding the reach of one's public interventions is not an easy proposition. Aside from institutional expectations and cultures, constant attacks on critical thinking and double standards of free speech in liberal democracies put additional pressures on public scholarship. Communication scholarship needs to ponder strategic responses to material, political, and socio-cultural challenges, including raising awareness about conditions, defending universities as autonomous spaces for critical thinking, and engaging with publics beyond the classroom.

4

Positions

How do communication scholars practice public scholarship? What roles do they take? In what way do they contribute to society? What normative commitments underpin their work? In this chapter I discuss the positions of public scholarship, which refers to both roles and their normative grounding.

Roles

As any expert in groups and organizations would tell you, roles are not just the reflection of personal impulses and inspirations: what individuals want to do in certain places and institutions. Positions reflect the negotiation between individuals and collective actors. This applies to public scholars, too. Roles are shaped at the intersection between personal motivations and institutional contexts, individual desires and organizational structures and dynamics. This is what Patrick Baert (2012) calls "agents and contexts" in his theory of intellectual positioning. One may believe that communication scholarship is and should be intertwined with applied work or politics, but actual positions are contingent on the interaction with specific publics: the relationship with communities of practice, policy-makers, and social movements that results from interaction and negotiation. If public scholarship is about public connections, roles represent the nodes between personal and institutional processes.

Communication scholars may take five roles in their public scholarship: practitioners, experts, activists, advocates, and commentators. These roles are ideal types that describe the interaction between scholars' expectations and communities' needs and expectations. They represent the dynamic relationship between scholars' contributions and public needs in specific institutional spaces and circumstances.

Scholar-practitioners are scholars who hold academic positions and work in other capacities outside the classroom and their research. They are documentarians, producers, journalists, writers, community mobilizers, immigration advocates, and health counselors. They hold dual passports as citizens of research and practice. They have skills and credentials that both researchers and practitioners recognize and praise. They blend practical and scholarly talents. They smudge the borders between scholarship and practice as they feed each other. They refuse to recognize academic scholarship as the bastion of knowledge purity; instead, they embrace knowledge as a porous endeavor that demands familiarity with the needs and skills of practitioners as well as the heft of scholarly research.

Scholar-experts collaborate with institutions on a particular area of inquiry and action. They work with government agencies, foundations, NGOs, and corporations to provide expert knowledge on various issues: research (design, data collection and analysis, monitoring and evaluation); message design for public health campaigns; training and curriculum development for educational programs; writing policy briefs for government agencies and donors. Communication scholars lend their expertise to institutions and publics interested primarily in rigorous, evidence-based approaches to develop and refine programmatic objectives and plans.

The expert model of public scholarship is grounded in the scientific model of value neutrality: the separation between knowledge and personal politics. Scholars work in their capacity as scientific experts with deep knowledge, methodological rigor, and other competencies. They need to be cognizant of the needs and objectives of other institutions, and speak their language to make themselves relevant. Experts generally work on initiatives that get (or try to build) support across partisan and ideological camps. One can think of issues such as children's media literacy, public interest media, specific public health campaigns (e.g. health literacy, flu prevention, cancer awareness) as examples of cross-ideological causes within specific circumstances and contexts. They reflect the power of issue coalitions interested in building common ground and locating partisan politics at a distance.

Expert interventions, however, are not depoliticized. Just because they are generally grounded in the normative neutrality of the scientific model, it does not mean they are apolitical. Contributing expertise to message design for tobacco control campaigns; community dialogue to destigmatize specific diseases; peace, environmental, and gendered-perspective reporting; media literacy for schoolchildren – all these are political activities. Moreover, where these issues are hotly debated and conflictive, their political dimensions become unavoidable. Even if scholars wish to remain in their role as experts, their positions may be construed as political.

Scholar-activists utilize academic expertise and/or publicly champion specific issues and political positions. They conceive academic knowledge as intertwined with political commitments. They dismiss the positivist ambition of removing personal subjectivity and politics from knowledge production. They claim ideology is always present in scholarship: in the selection of subjects of study, the position taken vis-à-vis the issues, and the purpose of research. They embrace clear ideological and ethical premises to reassert specific goals and combat a range of social ills: capitalism, racism, misogyny, exploitation, xenophobia, hatred, war. Scholar activism is not a solitary pursuit; rather, it is embedded in organized collective action.

Academic activism is not only associated with specific political goals: let's say, social justice or the end of capitalism (Carragee & Frey, 2016). Certainly, it has been often identified with radical and progressive models of intellectualism. Gramsci's notion of "organic intellectual" and Sartre's brand of intellectual *engagé* stand as prominent examples of this tradition (Baert, 2015). Academic activism, however, should not only be identified with involvement with a specific set of social classes, politics, or ideologies. Nor should it only be identified with particular tasks associated with certain ideological constructions of the "good intellectual," such as participating in the revolutionary vanguard in the struggle for cultural transformation or leading conservative reaction.

Instead, activism *tout court* is a form of engagement that embraces subjectivity, ideology, and politics and rejects the positivist canon of detached knowledge. It may pursue many ideological commitments and goals: radical, liberal, progressive, conservative. It can also be articulated with movements pursuing social justice on various fronts: voting rights, social equality, civic participation, legal status of migrants, access to health services.

Notwithstanding obstacles and pressures (Flood, Martin & Dreher, 2013), academic activists contribute by documenting problems, advocating for opportunities and solutions, championing specific interventions, and utilizing communication techniques to raise awareness and promote critical assessments, among other goals.

Scholar-advocates marry scholarly expertise with the open social and political commitment of scholar-activists. They lend their expert knowledge in collaborations with communities on myriad issues: environmental health, women's empowerment, migrants' rights, digital access among low-income communities. Yet they openly take political stands in favor of certain political goals: sustainable development, women's rights, access to jobs and citizenship. They neither hide their political sympathies nor only provide academic expertise. They advocate for specific changes, whether in their scholarly work or through connecting communities to opportunities and networks.

However, they are not activists, even if they feel closely identified with specific communities. Unlike activists, they are not embedded in communities. This is due to various reasons, including distance, difficult logistics, limited time, and academic obligations. It is hard to be an activist when one's everyday life is shaped by academic routines and expectations rather than by day-to-day events in specific communities. Research is also not only driven by activists' strategic priorities or ideological communion. It is also grounded in academic questions and primarily produced for academic publics.

Scholar-commentators occupy the position conventionally identified with the role of public intellectual: offering learned commentary about the issues of the day on the news media. Opportunities to do so have dramatically expanded with the proliferation of digital platforms. On the one hand, the ubiquity of digital communication and the media's fascination with a range of related subjects (from smartphone use among children to the impact of the Internet on democratic politics) have increased demand for expert opinion on a host of issues at the center of contemporary communication scholarship. On the other hand, the Internet has radically changed the politics of publicity, just as the media transformed the question of visibility in politics (Thompson, 2005). That is, scholarship can be publicized in many spaces and formats beyond the traditional sites of academia. Scholars can use various digital platforms to make their work and opinions publicly known without waiting for those occasional interviews and appearances in the legacy media.

Media fragmentation has chipped away at the model of the intellectual prophet whose power largely resided in having frequent access to a once limited resource: the media. Blogs, social media postings, filmed lectures, podcasts, YouTube channels, TED Talks, and many other platforms offer easy-to-access avenues for scholar-commentators. Certainly, the long tail of digital audiences does not mean that all platformed punditry reaches similar numbers of people. Many platforms offer plenty of immediate, unfiltered, and constant opportunities for commentators to express their views. This kind of engagement has become strongly encouraged by universities, publishers, and fellow academics (Gibson & Lipton, 2015; Pearce, 2015; Stein & Daniels, 2017).

Digital platforms are hospitable to different sets of competencies. Blogs and podcasts are open-ended in terms of style, duration, and format. Other platforms reward different, specific skills: Twitter welcomes sharp, snarky, humorous aphorisms; TED Talk rewards informative, entertaining, visually appealing lectures; YouTube is home to, well, everything; Instagram favors self-display, oversharing, and visual tidbits – all this is a far cry from the florid, esoteric language of highbrow public intellectuals of yore.

Just as it increases opportunities for public commentary, digital punditry has risks, too. It increases chances of surveillance and vitriol. Female and minority scholars as well as scholars who challenge multiple forms of power (e.g. whiteness, misogyny, militarism, imperialism) are more likely to meet the fury of the forces of hate. Trolls are ready to pounce. Scholars and universities are just beginning to come to terms with the consequences of digital publicity and digital speech. Exposure to one's ideas, especially if critical of reactionary forces, may bring about hate speech, shaming, and doxing. Universities love to promote faculty accomplishments, but they worry when media appearances devolve into public outcries.

The five positions here outlined aren't mutually exclusive, discrete, or static. They are possible, fluid options that describe the ways scholars engage with various publics. In these positions, scholars are members of collaborative endeavors. The exception is freewheeling commentary in blogs and other platforms, which isn't bounded by institutional considerations and rules. Public scholars need to be bilingual to straddle academic and public positions successfully. Among many other actions, they produce knowledge, translate academic research into the vernacular of specific non-academic actors, teach, develop curricula, draft proposals, and give testimony.

No position is better suited for addressing contemporary communication and social challenges. Different positions may make valuable contributions to addressing real-world problems as they intervene in different spaces. Addressing the communication and social problems previously mentioned demands various competencies of communication scholars: the practical skills of practitioners, the technical and research knowledge of experts, the commitment of activists, the bridging and strategic skills of advocates, and the written and oratory skills of commentators.

Positions are strategic as they depend on circumstances, opportunities, and obstacles. Therefore, a flexible approach is necessary, one that is sensitive to opportunities as well as politically astute. Positions are not free-floating, individual choices, but embedded in institutional opportunities and the needs of specific publics.

The main lesson from multiple positions and opportunities is that we should not associate public scholarship only with public intellectuals. Although some public intellectuals make important contributions by spreading knowledge and popularizing scholarly ideas among large publics, they are only one possible position. There are plenty of needs for public engagement beyond the literary/media sphere, the traditional home of the public intellectual, even if they are rarely in the media spotlight or attract public attention. Public scholarship makes important contributions in different roles and capacities. To broaden the conversation about and the perception of the manifold forms of public engagement, it is necessary to make them visible.

Normative positions

What about normative positions? Communication scholarship as well as the considerable literature on public scholarship has long wrestled with questions about the normative purpose of the intellectual enterprise. What are the political obligations of scholars? Should scholarship be administrative or critical? Should it collaborate with power or support subaltern actors? Should it help liberal democracy or promote radical change? Should it pursue objective knowledge or openly recognize subjectivity? Should it pierce the lies of governments and corporations? Tolstoy's famous provocation, as cited by Weber (1946, p. 153), among others, is relevant to these questions: "Science is meaningless because it gives no answer to our question, the only question important for us: 'What shall we do, and how shall we live?'"

Public scholarship reflects personal answers to these questions: the purpose of scholarship, the politics of one's work, the obligations to society, the relations between science and politics. As is to be expected, however, the answers are not unanimous. Public scholarship covers too much ground and comprises too many roles to be unified around

84

a common set of principles. No single normative model can infuse multiple forms of public
scholarship. One can do it for good or evil, to
support abstract human values or concrete forms
of social justice, to promote scientific progress or
revolutionary goals. The modern history of the
involvement of intellectuals and academics in
public life attests to the huge diversity of actions
and purposes entailed (Desch, 2016). There is
nothing intrinsically noble or redeeming about it.
It depends on the objectives and the guiding principles of public interventions.

My preferences are as follows. Public scholarship
needs to be guided by core principles of both the
academic enterprise (truth-telling, evidence, rigor,
rationality) and democratic progressivism (account-
ability, tolerance, empathy, solidarity, social justice).
It needs to espouse critical rationality and remain
wary of power in its multiple manifestations. It
needs to offer evidence-based reasoning for understanding and addressing communication and social
problems. It needs to take a constructive position to
contribute to public life and social justice. It should
be intellectually open to permanently think about
the relationship between research and practice. It
needs to be strategic by identifying opportunities
and allies for social change.

Public scholars need to be critics in the sense defined by Edward Said (1994, p. 11): those "whose place it is publicly to raise embarrassing questions, to confront orthodoxy and dogma (rather than to produce them)," and "who cannot easily be co-opted by governments or corporations." It's the scholar who capitalizes on public presence to challenge convictions, champion counter-publics, and raise controversy. "Speaking truth to power" is the north star of the critic (Keren & Hawkins, 2015). Critics express what is unexpected – the ideas that shake up conventional wisdom, regardless of the issue or ideological underpinnings. Critics remain anti-dogmatic and try to stay autonomous or, minimally, at a healthy distance from particular interests. Critics remind society about unexpected, counterintuitive ideas (Hirschman, 1981). Critics are not afraid of taking marginal, contrarian positions to challenge conventional wisdom and bring up uncomfortable positions. Critics can be inspired by a scientific approach that upholds "organized skepticism" (Merton, 1973) as a central disposition, or by the politics of public reason against all forms of power. Critics can be free agents or work with counter-publics (Burawoy, 2005).

Holding a critical disposition is central to truth-telling: to denounce lies and inconvenient facts that power prefers to keep secret. Power easily becomes tone-deaf to reality; it is prone to stifle criticism and to seek constant acclaim. Too close to power, public scholarship devolves into sycophancy: producing self-flattering ideas and empty niceties out of loyalty to the regime, bowing to Dear Leaders, justifying murderous doctrines and actions, or ignoring human rights violations. *Realpolitik* calculations, blind ideological communion, and money blunt the potential sharp edge of public scholarship. Public scholars should not look the other way in the face of authoritarianism, no matter what the ideological bent or crass justification.

Public scholars should offer constructive reasoning to address and resolve communication and social problems. Constructive reasoning is fundamental to assess problems, solutions, and interests. Intellectual gadflies and pugilists who subvert conventional wisdom and lob brickbats from their academic perch may not add much to collective action for social good. Dressing down power is only one step towards the arduous construction of more just societies.

Constructive reasoning needs to tap into a trove of communication scholarship: evidence-based arguments for understanding communication problems and proposing courses of action. This is our added value – what no other group or institution offers. We help publics understand communication phenomena by publishing and discussing research findings. We can explain the value of democratic practices: negotiation, engagement, listening, understanding, tolerance. We know the impact of different forms of communication to tackle social problems. We bring up a sense of historical proportion and global awareness grounded in past studies to help societies understand current communication challenges and options. This knowledge needs to be mobilized when scholars express ideas that are not heard, foster debates, embrace non-conformism, revisit received knowledge, and ask the right questions.

Public scholarship should be open to revisiting research and practice. Just as scholarly research contributes to social practice, public scholarship enriches research. It serves as a reality check for theoretical arguments, empirical conclusions, and analytical frameworks. As an interstitial form of knowledge production, public scholarship is at the cross-flows of different ideas. Practical engagement infuses news ideas and pushes us to rethink research. It helps us to contextualize, enrich, understand, clarify, and interrogate scholarly agendas, interests, and priorities. This is especially necessary as scholarship dealing with real-world problems oftentimes devolves into pure intellectual exercises for fellow academics rather than being engaged with actual contexts of practice and everyday public concerns and orienting itself towards infusing actions that bring about social change.

As we interact with others, our perspectives vis-à-vis our own work and our area of inquiry shift. We realize that what publics need is not always aligned with what scholarship considers urgent or important. Perhaps too much attention is given to topics that, although they are intellectually stimulating, are not relevant to people's lives and social change. We may conclude that areas of research don't need yet another study on topics that have been exhaustively investigated and that, instead, we need studies that inform practice. We may need a better understanding of successful strategies to change media representations, news coverage, Internet access and use (rather than conducting new studies proving what we already suspect). Public scholarship may also steer research agendas in the direction of real-world problem studies. It may help to identify research gaps. It may bring citizens' concerns to the center of research. It may help to figure out how various publics (e.g. parents, migrants, voters, children, journalists) at the center of communication studies react to our arguments and language. We may realize that we have competencies to support social change in other ways: listening, moderating, sharing knowledge, facilitating learning.

To take full advantage of the cross-pollination between research and practice, we should be open-minded and committed to intellectual flexibility. When dealing with real-world problems, having ready-made, foolproof questions and answers does not serve us well for we may be blinded to recognizing different challenges, opportunities, and solutions. Theoretical and ideological dogmatism leads to holding the proverbial hammer that sees all problems as nails. Given the range of communication and social problems, across settings and scenarios, we need to be intellectually nimble to let reality refine or change our perspective.

In summary, public scholarship in communication studies should espouse critical, constructive reasoning. It needs to be skeptical of power, dogmatism, and ideology. It should foreground essential aspects of the scholarly enterprise: facts and rigor, general propositions and unique insights, history and perspective.

5

Proposals

Before outlining my proposal for future actions, let's summarize the arguments presented.

First, we need to shift the perspective on public scholarship. Public scholarship in communication studies takes place where publics live and work. It is limited neither to the high priests of public intellectualism nor to the arena of the media. If we broaden our understanding of public scholarship, mourning the passing of the "public intellectual" is unnecessary. The era of "mega public intellectuals" may be over (Drezner, 2009), as observers (Herman, 2017; Mitchell, 2017) lament. If one scans the mainstream media for highbrow television shows and long-format magazines, one could nostalgically conclude that towering intellectual giants are a dying breed. But we need to look for public scholarship beyond the media and in other public spaces. We need to direct attention to the sites where groups, networks, and "knowledge clubs" (Hartley, 2015) engage with social problems and practical questions. If we take a broader conception of public spaces and public knowledge (Dahlgren 2012), then we find that public scholarship is flourishing.

Communication scholars have worked with states, international organizations, civic society organizations, political parties, unions, neighborhood associations, and schools. They have collaborated to support a wide range of goals: news/media literacy, gender equality, critical dialogue and thinking, quality news, communication rights, environmental health, grassroots media, community empowerment, inter-group tolerance, diversity in media representation, minority rights, freedom of expression, public communication policies, healthier lives, Internet participation. They have served in different positions by producing content, contributing insights from research, developing and testing interventions, assessing results, providing expert testimonies, advocating for issues. There are public interventions in a wide range of public spaces, even though they are often neglected in a mindset inclined to recognize only mediated scholarship as public scholarship.

Second, we need to recognize and to support

various forms of public scholarship. To do this, we need to open the lens to view the multiple connections between communication scholarship and society. Just as public spaces change, new forms of organization, expression, and action emerge, too. There is no single path or form of public scholarship. Scholars and universities develop and cultivate relationships with a range of publics and spaces: neighborhoods, communities of practice, problem-oriented alliances. Multifaceted spaces of interventions and forms of collaborations attest to the vibrancy and the diversity of public scholarship. We need to recognize how scholars use their expertise to serve multiple publics while attending to standard academic expectations.

Unfortunately, the presence and the impact of public scholarship is not always sufficiently recognized in communication studies. At best, it is considered a specialty: as an area of interest under various names (e.g. applied, activist, social justice) rather than as a normative vision that should cross all areas of work. As part of the mission of communication scholarship, we should recognize multifaceted interventions that contribute to the public good and inform teaching and research.

A key problem is that neither universities nor academic cultures give enough credit to public scholarship (Doberneck, Glass & Schweitzer, 2010). They rarely recognize its significance even if they embrace the rhetoric about the importance of public service. Rhetoric is not enough to strengthen socially oriented work. In fact, many colleagues "wait" to do public scholarship until they have job security because they are told it doesn't count for tenure. The boundless promises of public scholarship are tempered by the realities and the politics of academia: namely the ambivalent support of academic and professional institutions. Given these obstacles, it is not surprising that public scholarship largely rides on the personal passion of scholars willing to do the "double shift" of scholarship and public scholarship.

These challenges take us to the inevitable question of any manifesto: what needs to be done?

What is needed are sustainable, multi-pronged efforts to persuade universities to recognize different forms of public engagement as an integral part of communication studies. It is necessary to broaden the basis of support beyond scholars convinced that public scholarship matters. Preaching to the choir is not enough to make further inroads. Talk among people already convinced about public scholarship will not move things far.

We need to build a groundswell of support for

public scholarship with key goals: reward and support different types of situations and choices, accommodate multiple intellectual identities and scholarly trajectories, and be more open and inclusive of different visions about the purpose of communication studies – a dynamic, shapeshifting post-discipline at the intersection of research and practice. Be strategic: build a movement, broaden support, define objectives, identify opportunities.

Public scholarship demands more than impassioned, inspiring appeals to the public-mindedness of scholars. Rousing calls may not yield tangible results as long as institutional expectations and academic cultures limit or do not encourage individual interest. Just calling for communication scholars to practice public scholarship sounds glib without clear actions to address tangible institutional conditions: the systems of recognition and incentives that shape academic decisions. We need to recognize myriad forms and spaces and drive the changes necessary to bolster public scholarship.

The challenge is to make public scholarship integral to scholarship. It should not be an add-on activity, performed during (imaginary) extra time, or as an eventual luxury after attaining job security. It should not be just a pat on our collective backs. It should be recognized and supported as emblematic of the best contributions of communication studies to society.

Should everyone practice public scholarship? No. Does it mean that we should be skeptical of speculative, "non-applied" research or "scholarship for scholars"? Not really. Various visions of communication scholarship are equally valuable. Intellectual wanderlusters, dyed-in-the-wool researchers, scientists with inscrutable politics, community champions, computational experts – all make significant contributions. Yet everyone should have opportunities to know the forms of public scholarship and learn the competencies it demands. Institutions should encourage students and faculty to know and embrace public scholarship.

Here are suggestions to strengthen public scholarship in communication studies at multiple levels: individual, institutional, and societal. These proposed actions are not intended to be universally valid – to be similarly relevant across settings. Notably, there are vast differences across settings in terms of the economic and political situation in public and private universities; the historical nexus between academia and local politics; the conditions for unfettered speech and critical thinking; university expectations about performance; national intellectual traditions; and socio-political junctures.

Take the case of universities. Unlike the relatively peaceful situation in most universities in the global North, elsewhere the situation is different. In recent years, governments with a terrible human rights record have continued to crush universities in many countries (e.g. China, Egypt, Nicaragua, Turkey). They have raided and shut down campuses, and persecuted, arrested, tear-gassed, and fired dissident faculty and students. Not all universities are similarly (un)interested in promoting academic outreach: whereas some institutions have clear social missions and reward faculty who work with communities, others are determined to maximize faculty performance by imposing metrics that prioritize fund-raising records, publication output, and external activities that contribute to the bottom line. Public and private universities generally do not have similar mandates, and are bound by different obligations to taxpayers and relationships with governments.

Therefore, no common platform for public scholarship would be similarly relevant given considerable variations in academic settings as well as socio-political contexts.

Here I submit ideas for further actions.

Decide the public scholar you want to be

At the individual level, scholars need to determine expectations and search for opportunities. The impetus is personal rather than institutional. Many colleagues will remind you about publishing, teaching, and professional service expectations; fewer colleagues, however, will remind you to be an academic citizen in your community. So, if you believe the fulfilled life includes public scholarship, you need to choose the kind of public scholar you want to be. Decide what difference you want to make in society and why. Make yourself useful and relevant to non-academic publics. Figure out what skills you need and why. Select a public problem, find partners, build trust, understand needs and expectations, be clear about your interests and commitments. Think about how you can help various communities of belonging. Document practices, experiences, and lessons. Nurture networks. Explain what you do to colleagues and university administrators in such a way that they understand your contributions to academia and the public. Connect with other public scholars. Rethink scholarly questions on the basis of your practical experiences.

Bolster public scholarship in both universities and scholarly cultures

At the institutional level, a twofold approach is needed.

Work to improve institutional conditions in universities

Think about the how national public policies that promote public scholarship, such as Canada's initiative for "knowledge mobilization," are relevant to your university and country. Learn from virtuous cases of universities committed to recognizing and encouraging faculty to get involved through institutes dedicated to public scholarship, maintaining active partnerships around specific real-world problems with non-academic actors, offering funding support, and incorporating relevant metrics in annual reports and tenure and promotion packages. Learn from how universities with a social justice mission translate ideals into effective actions and assess impact. Set up centers that provide spaces, funding, and assistance to help scholars connect with non-academic communities. Ease up protocols to get Institutional Review Board approvals (coordinating and getting permissions from non-academic actors generally is already challenging). Don't shy away from supporting action-oriented scholarship, especially on controversial issues that make administrators reach for their dyspepsia pills and university boards forgo their commitment to free speech. Collaborate with state agencies as well as public and private funders to promote public scholarship through grants that demand universities collaborate with other actors on communication and social problems. Work with universities to offer training in public scholarship beyond conventional media skills: invite suggestions, offer incentives to develop new partnerships, offer opportunities to improve competencies. Expand ways to recognize scholarly performance beyond the traditional academic publications such as multimedia artifacts produced in partnership with non-academic actors. Change the ways universities recognize the impact of scholarship beyond conventional metrics (citations, awards, media mentions). Advocate in support of the relevance of public scholarship. Make room for various forms of scholarship. Elevate the profile of "knowledge mobilization" initiatives on campus. Recognize various forms of public scholarship. Find allies among university presidents, provosts, deans, and colleagues to bolster the recognition of public scholarship. Refine ways to understand and assess the impact of public scholarship. In summary, work to make public scholarship a logical outgrowth of intellectual work rather than a daring move that can imperil academic careers or tarnish the reputation of scholars as being not truly committed to the scientific enterprise. Find out if your university takes part in community engagement programs (such as the Carnegie Engaged University in the United States) or if there are similar initiatives by private foundations and governments, and collaborate with colleagues across campus to bolster the presence of public scholarship.

Make academic cultures supportive of public scholarship

Here the challenge is to raise awareness about the multiple forms of public scholarship in standard academic platforms: publications, panels, professional associations, awards. Change the perception that public scholars are media mavens, and that they often water down complex ideas for mass consumption. Incorporate public scholarship in the mechanisms used to assess, evaluate, and recognize scholarly work. Give platforms to an array of public scholars to share their work and bring their partners into academic spaces. Promote cross-cutting collaborations among public scholars to address communication and social problems. Remind colleagues to ask why research matters and demonstrate with impact evidence. Document and share experiences from across the vast landscape of communication studies. Produce comparative analysis of public scholarship around the world. Foster global networks to promote collaboration and exchanges. Produce data to demonstrate the contributions of public scholarship. Help to dispel the notion that public scholarship is not rigorous by offering evidence-based arguments about its contributions to scholarship and society. Tell skeptics why public scholarship matters. Understand their reservations and show ways to address their concerns. Demonstrate the compatibility between public scholarship and excellent scholarship. Work with funders to recognize public scholarship in grant applications and performance evaluation; in turn, partner with funders who want to be champions of public scholarship to work with university administrators.

Foster socio-political conditions for autonomous public scholarship

At the societal level, the main task is to support public scholarship when political circumstances endanger interventions in support of democracy and social justice. Authoritarian governments blunt the potential edge and the social mission of public scholarship through multiple mechanisms: defunding public universities with a reputation for politically and socially committed scholarship and mission; persecuting dissenting scholars with a significant public presence; excluding critical scholarship from public funding agencies; pressuring university officials and benefactors. The problems for public scholarship committed to social justice are similar in different countries ruled by reactionary forces. Regardless of the characteristics of the political regime or its avowed ideological sympathies, those forces share common attributes: instinctive distrust of critical thinking; a tendency to eviscerate autonomous spaces for scholarship and action; opposition to independent NGOs and grassroots associations; the labeling of critics as traitors, enemies, and foreign agents; and the utilizing of overt and covert mechanisms to weaken public scholarship committed to facts and truth-telling.

Undoubtedly, the ideas set out above are a tall order. But nobody said public scholarship is easy. Without sustainable institutional and socio-political changes, public scholarship will not become firmly embedded in academic life – recognized and supported as a contribution of rigorous knowledge to public life and social justice. Paeans to public scholarship are symbolically important. Stirring language, however, needs to be translated into effective actions for improving institutional conditions and addressing obstacles. Unless lofty rhetoric is accompanied by concrete changes, it may have as much impact as get-well cards on personal health or commencement speeches on world peace.

We need to bring insights from lab experiments, surveys, ethnographies, and content analysis to publics who may benefit in multiple ways: understanding problems, promoting positive change, overturning anti-social decisions and policies, becoming educated about the dizzying forces of contemporary digital societies. We need to strengthen public scholarship to attend to expectations by students and parents about employment and the real-world contributions of education and research, and to meet funders' expectations about the public impact of research grants. We need to practice public scholarship, too, to assess the generalizability, relevance, and solidity of findings and arguments of our scholarship to real-world problems.

Public scholarship demands a reflexive perspective on the purpose of communication studies – one that interrogates its mission, broadens intellectual horizons and spaces of interventions, situates the academic enterprise in historical-social contexts, and cares about who benefits from our work.

References

Ali, C., & Herzog, C. (2018). From praxis to pragmatism: Junior scholars and policy impact. *The Communication Review*. Retrieved from *https://doi.org/10.1080/10714421.2018.1492284*

Arendt, H. (1958). *The human condition*. Chicago: University of Chicago Press.

Baert, P. (2012). Positioning theory and intellectual interventions. *Journal for the Theory of Social Behaviour*, *42*(3), 304–324.

Baert, P. (2015). *The existentialist moment: The rise of Sartre as a public intellectual*. New York: John Wiley & Sons.

Barthes, R. (1972). *Mythologies* (A. Lavers, Trans.). New York: Hill & Wang.

Basnyat, I. (2019). Self-reflexivity for social change: The researcher, I, and the researched, female street-based commercial sex workers,' gendered contexts. In M. Dutta & D. Zapata (Eds.), *Communicating*

References

for social change (pp. 13–31). Singapore: Palgrave Macmillan US.

Bastow, S., Dunleavy, P., & Tinkler, J. (2014). *The impact of the social sciences: How academics and their research make a difference.* London: Sage.

Bourdieu, P. (2008). *Political interventions: Social science and political action* (F. Poupeau & T. Discepolo, Eds.; D. Fernbach, Trans.). London: Verso.

Buckingham, D. (2013). Representing audiences: Audience research, public knowledge, and policy. *The Communication Review*, *16*(1–2), 51–60.

Burawoy, M. (2005). For public sociology. *American Sociological Review*, *70*(1), 4–28.

Burgess, R. (1988). Conversations with a purpose: The ethnographic interview in educational research. *Studies in Qualitative Methodology, 1*, 137–155.

Calhoun, C. (2004). Toward a more public social science. *Items and Issues*, *5*(1–2), 4–5.

Calhoun, C. (2006). The university and the public good. *Thesis Eleven*, *84*(1), 7–43.

Canella, G. (2016). CAP! Comcast: The framing and distribution strategies of policy advocates within networked communications. *International Journal of Communication*, *10*, 5889–5907.

Carragee, K. M., & Frey, L. R. (2016). Communication activism research: Engaged communication scholarship for social justice. *International Journal of Communication*, *10*, 3975–3999.

References

Collier, M. J., & Lawless, B. (2016). Critically reflexive dialogue and praxis: Academic/practitioner reflections throughout a formative evaluation of Circles® USA. *Journal of Applied Communication Research*, 44(2), 156–173.

Couldry, N., & Hepp, A. (2016). *The mediated construction of reality*. Cambridge: Polity.

Dahlgren, P. (2012). Public intellectuals, online media, and public spheres: Current realignments. *International Journal of Politics, Culture, and Society*, 25(4), 95–110.

Dempsey, S., Dutta, M., Frey, L. R., Goodall, H. L., Madison, D. S., Mercieca, J., Nakayama, T., & Miller, K. (2011). What is the role of the communication discipline in social justice, community engagement, and public scholarship? A visit to the CM Café. *Communication Monographs*, 78(2), 256–271.

Desch, M. C. (Ed.). (2016). *Public intellectuals in the global arena: Professors or pundits?* South Bend, IN: University of Notre Dame Press.

Doberneck, D. M., Glass, C. R., & Schweitzer, J. (2010). From rhetoric to reality: A typology of publically engaged scholarship. *Journal of Higher Education Outreach and Engagement, 14*(4), 5–35.

Drezner, D. W. (2009). Public Intellectuals 2.1. *Society*, 46(1), 49–54.

Eagleton, T. (2017, May 26). Terry Eagleton: A lit crit of the party manifestos. *The Guardian*. Retrieved from

References

*https://www.theguardian.com/books/2017/may/26/
terry-eagleton-a-lit-crit-of-the-party-manifestos*

Eckert, S., & Steiner, L. (2018). Teaching girls online skills for knowledge projects: A research-based feminist intervention. In D. Harp, J. Loke, & I. Bachmann (Eds.), *Feminist approaches to media theory and research* (pp. 219–235). Cham: Palgrave Macmillan.

Eckert, S., Metzger-Riftkin, J., & Nurmis, J. (2018). Teaching girls online skills: Results of the Wikid Grrls intervention. *Journal of Media Literacy Education*,*10*(3), 20–42.

Flinders, M. (2013). The tyranny of relevance and the art of translation. *Political Studies Review*, *11*(2), 149–167.

Flood, M., Martin, B., & Dreher, T. (2013). Combining academia and activism: Common obstacles and useful tools. *Australian Universities Review*, *55*(1), 17–26.

Frey, L. R., & Palmer, D. L. (2017). Communication activism pedagogy and research: Communication education scholarship to promote social justice. *Communication Education*, *66*(3), 362–367.

Garnham, N. (1990). *Capitalism and communication*. London: Sage.

Gibson, T., & Lipton, M. (2015). *Research, write, create: Connecting scholarship and digital media*. Toronto: Oxford University Press.

Habermas, J. (1989). *The structural transformation of the public sphere: An inquiry into a category of*

References

bourgeois society (T. Burger, Trans.). Cambridge, MA: MIT Press.

Hanemaayer, A., & Schneider, C. J. (2015). *The public sociology debate*. Vancouver: UBC Press.

Hartley, J. (2015). Public intellectuals: *La lutte continue?* *Media International Australia*, *156*(1), 108–122.

Herman, D. (2017, January 31). Whatever happened to the public intellectual? *New Statesman*. Retrieved from *http://www.newstatesman.com/culture/books/2017/01/whatever-happened-public-intellectual*

Hirschman, A. (1981). *Essays in trespassing: Economics to politics and beyond*. New York: Cambridge University Press.

Hoffman, A. J. (2016). Reflections: Academia's emerging crisis of relevance and the consequent role of the engaged scholar. *Journal of Change Management*, *16*(2) 77–96.

Hofstadter, R. (1963). *Anti-intellectualism in American life*. New York: Vintage.

Jacoby, R. (1987). *The last intellectuals: American culture in the age of academe*. New York: Basic Books.

Jacoby, R. (2015, November 29). The latest intellectuals. *The Chronicle of Higher Education*. Retrieved from *https://www.chronicle.com/article/The-Latest-Intellectuals/234339?cid=cp16*

Judt, T. (1992). *Past imperfect: French intellectuals, 1944–1956*. Berkeley: University of California Press.

Katz, V. S., & Gonzalez, C. (2016). Toward meaningful connectivity: Using multilevel communication research to reframe digital inequality. *Journal of Communication*, 66(2), 236–249.

Keren, M., & Hawkins, R. (2015). *Speaking power to truth: Digital discourse and the public intellectual*. Edmonton: AU Press.

Kolucki, B., & Lemish, D. (2011). *Communicating with children*. New York: UNICEF.

Kristof, N. (2014, February 15). Professors, we need you! *New York Times*. Retrieved from *https://www.nytimes.com/2014/02/16/opinion/sunday/kristof-professors-we-need-you.html*

Lentz, B. (2014a). The media policy tower of babble: A case for "policy literacy pedagogy". *Critical Studies in Media Communication*, 31(2), 134–140.

Lentz, B. (2014b). Building the pipeline of media and technology policy advocates: The role of "situated learning". *Journal of Information Policy*, 4, 176–204.

Livingstone, S., Burton, P., Cabello, P., Helsper, E., Kanchev, P., Kardefelt-Winther, D., Perovic, J., Stoilova, M., & Ssu-Han, Y. (2017). *Media and information literacy among children on three continents: Insights into the measurement and mediation of well-being*. Paris: UNESCO.

Mannheim, K. (1936). *Ideology and utopia: An introduction to the sociology of knowledge*. New York: Harvest.

Marwick A. E. (2013). *Status update: Celebrity, publicity, and branding in the social media age*. New Haven, CT: Yale University Press.

References

Merton, R. (1973). The normative structure of science. In N. W. Storer (Ed.), *The sociology of science: Theoretical and empirical investigations* (pp. 267–278). Chicago: University of Chicago Press.

Miller, N. (1999). *In the shadow of the state: Intellectuals and the quest for national identity in twentieth-century Spanish America.* New York: Verso.

Mitchell, E. (2017, July 1). What happened to America's public intellectuals? *Smithsonian Magazine.* Retrieved from *https://www.smithsonianmag.com/history/what-happened-americas-public-intellectuals-180963668/#oo5ZCbv1puXfS6IQ.99*

Mulholland, J. (2015, December 10). Academics: Forget about public engagement, stay in your ivory towers. *The Guardian.* Retrieved from *https://www.theguardian.com/higher-education-network/2015/dec/10/academics-forget-about-public-engagement-stay-in-your-ivory-towers*

Napoli, P. M., Stonbely, S., McCollough, K., & Renninger, B. (2017). Local journalism and the information needs of local communities: Toward a scalable assessment approach. *Journalism Practice, 11*(4), 373–395.

Nielsen, R. K. (2018). No one cares what we know: Three responses to the irrelevance of political communication research. *Political Communication, 35*(1), 145–149.

Oakes, J. (2018). 2016 AERA Presidential Address: Public scholarship: education research for a diverse democracy. *Educational Researcher, 47*(2), 91–104.

References

Orwell, G. (1968). *The collected essays, journalism and letters of George Orwell* (S. Orwell & I. Angus,Eds.). London: Secker & Warburg.

Palma, K. (2015). The nation and the domestic: A performance about feminism and praxis in the Chilean Andes. *Qualitative Inquiry, 21*(8), 696–703.

Pearce, K. E. (2015). Counting to nowhere: Social media adoption and use as an opportunity for public scholarship and engagement. *Social Media + Society, 1*(1). Retrieved from *https://doi.org/10.1177/2056305115 578672*

Peters, G., Pierre, J., & Stoker, G. (2014). *The relevance of political science.* New York: Palgrave Macmillan

Posner, R. A. (2002). *Public intellectuals: A study of decline.* Cambridge, MA: Harvard University Press.

The Provost's Committee on University Outreach. (1993). *University Outreach at Michigan State University: Extending Knowledge to Serve Society* (Rep.). Michigan State University. Retrieved from *https://engage.msu.edu/upload/documents-reports/Pro vostCommitteeReport_2009ed.pdf*

Ricci, D. (1987). *The tragedy of political science: Politics, scholarship, and democracy.* New Haven, CT: Yale University Press.

Román-Velázquez, P. (2014). Claiming a place in the global city: Urban regeneration and Latin American spaces in London. *Revista Eptic, 16*(1), 68–83.

Robé, C., Wolfson, T., & Funke, P. N. (2016). Rewiring the apparatus: Screen theory, media activism, and working-class subjectivities. *Rethinking Marxism*, 28(1), 57–72.

Rosen J. (1995). Public journalism: A case for public scholarship. *Change*, 27(3), 34–38.

Said, E. W. (1994). *Representations of the intellectual: The 1993 Reith Lectures*. New York: Vintage.

Segura, M. S., & Waisbord, S. (2016). *Media movements*. London: Zed.

Smeltzer, S., & Cantillon, S. (2015). Guest editors' introduction II: Reflections on scholarship and activism in Canada and Ireland. *Studies in Social Justice*, 9(2), 136–141.

Smith, J. A., Lloyd, M., & Pickard, V. (2015). Communication in action: Bridging research and policy – introduction. *International Journal of Communication*, 9(3), 3411–3413.

Smith, S. L., Choueiti, M., & Pieper, K. (2016). Inclusion or invisibility? Comprehensive Annenberg report on diversity in entertainment. Institute for Diversity and Empowerment at Annenberg (IDEA): USC Annenberg School for Communication and Journalism. Retrieved from *https://annenberg.usc.edu/sites/default/files/2017/04/07/MDSCI_CARD_Report_FINAL_Exec_Summary.pdf*

Son, M., & Ball-Rokeach, S. (2016). The whole community communication infrastructure: The case of Los Angeles. In M. Lloyd & L. Friedland (Eds.), *The communication crisis in America, and how to fix it*. New York: Palgrave Macmillan.

References

Stein, A., & Daniels, J. (2017). *Going public: A guide for social scientists*. Chicago: University of Chicago Press.

Stroud, N. J. (2017). Helping newsrooms work toward their democratic and business objectives. In P. J. Boczkowski & C. W. Anderson (Eds.), *Remaking the news: Essays on the future of journalism scholarship in the digital age* (pp. 157–176). Cambridge, MA: MIT Press.

Thompson, J. B. (2005). The new visibility. *Theory, Culture & Society*, 22(6), 31–51.

Tzara, T. (1981). *Grains et issues*. Paris: Garnier-Flammarion.

Villanueva, G., González, C., Son, M., Moreno, E., Liu, W., & Ball-Rokeach, S. (2017). Bringing local voices into community revitalization: Engaged communication research in urban planning. *Journal of Applied Communication Research*, 45(5), 474–494.

Waisbord, S. (2014). United and fragmented: Communication and media studies in Latin America. *Journal of Latin American Communication Research*, 4(1), 55–77.

Waisbord, S. (2019). *Communication: A post-discipline*. Cambridge: Polity.

Washburn, J. (2005). *University, Inc.: The corporate corruption of higher education*. New York: Basic Books.

Weber, M. (1946). Science as a vocation. In H. H. Gerth & C. W. Mills (Eds.), *From Max Weber: Essays in sociology* (pp. 129–156). New York: Oxford University Press.

References

Wilkin, H. A. (2013). Exploring the potential of communication infrastructure theory for informing efforts to reduce health disparities. *Journal of Communication, 63*(1), 181–200.

Williams, J. J. (2018, August 5). The rise of the promotional intellectual. *The Chronicle of Higher Education.* Retrieved from *https://www.chronicle.com/article/The-Rise-of-the-Promotional/244135*

Wilson J. K. (2016). The changing media and academic freedom. *Academe, 102*(1), 8–12.

Wright, K. (2018). "Helping our beneficiaries tell their own stories?" International aid agencies and the politics of voice in news production. *Global Media and Communication, 14*(1), 85–102.

Zuckerberg, M. (2017, June 22). Bringing the world closer together. Facebook. Retrieved from *https://www.facebook.com/notes/mark-zuckerberg/bringing-the-world-closer-together/10154944663901634/*